NO SECOND CHANCES

A Family Guide to the College Decision and the Lasting Impact of Debt

DAVID BRADSHAW, CPA, MBA

No Second Chances – Copyright under: Your Debt + Your Degree = Your Future Destroyed: A Family Guide to the College Decision and the Lasting Impact of Debt.

http://www.keepyours.org

Book and Cover design by Designer

ISBN: 978-1-7373713-3-5

First Edition: July 2024

CONTENTS

THE AMERICAN DREAM **1**

INTRODUCTION **7**

Do We Expect Children to Make the Right Decisions? 10

PART 1 ..... **17**

GOOD INTENTIONS ON THE HERO'S JOURNEY **17**

The Debt Impact on Your Life 19
Not All Debt is the Same 21
The College Mobility Illusion 24
Why I Got Involved 32

PART 2 ..... **37**

THE 'WHY' OF COLLEGE **37**

The 'Why' Explored 39
Takeaways on 'Why' 48
Don't Forget the 'What' 49
The 'What' College Value Analysis 50
The 'What' of College Value Explored 52
Takeaways on the 'What' of College 56

PART 3 ..... **57**

LET'S LEARN ABOUT YOU! **57**

Learning About You Questions 64
Learning About You, Explored 66
Johnson O'Conner Aptitude Assessment 68
The Academic You 69
Exploring Your Academic Self 70
Takeaways on Learning about You 79

PART 4 ..... **80**

THE SYSTEM OF HIGHER EDUCATION **80**

The System of Higher Education, Explored 82
Takeaways from Exploring the System of Higher Education 99
Dirty Secrets that Universities Don't Want You to Know 100
Suckers Pay Retail 104
The Ranking System in Higher Education 112
The 'What' is More Important than the 'Where' 117
The Ivy League Proposition 118
The Ivy League Degree Mobility Illusion 122
Takeaways in the Dirty Secrets They Don't Want You to Know 126

PART 5 .... **127**

THE REAL COST OF COLLEGE **127**

Exploring the Real Cost of College 129
Out-of-State Tuition: The Worst Value of All 134
The Value of Scholarships and Grants 137
Takeaways in the Real Cost of College 138

PART 6 .... **139**

FAMILY FINANCES **139**

Alternative Use of Family Money 143
Takeaways in Family Finances 147
Stories of Family Finances 148

PART 7 .... **150**

HACKING THE SYSTEM **150**

No Debt Plan 1 – For Those Who Can Live at Home 152
No Debt Plan 2 – For Those Who Cannot Live at Home 154
Employers with Tuition Reimbursement: 156
The Value of Tuition Reimbursement 156
Housing Hacks 157
Federal Student Aid – Pell Grant Help 160
Takeaways on Hacking the System: 163

PART 8 .... **164**

FOUR CHOICES, FOUR LIVES 164
The Students' Choices 167
The Costs of Each Student's Choice 172
What College Choices Mean for Life After College......175
Takeaways from Choices 182

PART 9 183

THE TOTAL COST OF DEBT 183
Debt's Impact on Your Psyche......185
Debt's Hidden Burden – Job Choice 187
The Real Cost of Debt......189
The Value of Family Help 191
Takeaways on the Real Cost of Debt 194

PART 10 195

BUILDING YOUR PLAN 195
Everyone in the Family Do Their Part......199
Get a Head Start 201

PART 11 202

STRATEGIES FOR YOUR FAMILY SITUATION 202
No Family Support, Can't (Or Won't) Live at Home 203
Family Support For Living, But Not Tuition 205
Family Support for Living and Tuition 207
Family Situation, Final Thoughts 209
END OF BOOK NOTES 210

SUPPLEMENT 1 211

CONDENSED HISTORY OF STUDENT LOAN CRISIS 211

SUPPLEMENT 2 217

SPORTS AND COLLEGE 217
The Sports Partial Scholarship Value Proposition 223

SUPPLEMENT 3 227

THE FORMS...227

SUPPLEMENT 4 229

OUT-OF-STATE TUITION HACKS...229

FIXING THE CURRENT PROBLEM..234

ARTIFICIAL INTELLIGENCE IMPACTS TO EDUCATION.....................................241

The American Dream

The experiment that is America began in 1797 when George Washington decided not to become King of America, but instead, along with America's other founders, gave us the Constitution and the Bill of Rights Since the granting of liberty, free speech and the pursuit of happiness was enshrined, we have seen the greatest growth in the prosperity of the world in all of recorded history. Before the American Revolution, almost everyone in the world was a surf, subject to a King, Czar or some other totalitarian ruler. Whether you served the empire in its home state or a colony, fundamental human rights did not exist. Americans, generations of immigrants seeking a better life, have transformed the world with ingenuity and creativity, spawned by the individual rights guaranteed to us from the Constitution and Bill of Rights. The realization of this prosperity is colloquially known throughout the world as the American Dream.

Without America and entrepreneurship, the world would look very different. There may not be electricity, or it may have been reserved for the ruling class. All the additional technical innovations since would likely have been very muted. Women would not have equal rights, none of us would have individual freedom, private property, or equality before the law. Peace would be the exception instead of the norm. From electricity to the telegraph to cars and computers it has been American entrepreneurs leading the way. It is not a surprise that the iPhone and more recently Chat GPT came from American companies, it is instead the result of innovation allowed in the land of the free. There is a huge difference in the freedom that Elon Musk and Jeff Bezos have versus Jack Ma.

Before America, the ruling class was chosen by the King, and they were the only people with rights. They were not elected, and rarely was the choice made based on merit. Alternatively, the American dream was born out of meritocracy, offering great rewards for those who invent, innovate, and create value for us all. There is a reason Elon Musk came to America, it is a place where dreams can be turned into reality. New entrepreneurs continue to solve the world's problems and we need more of them to face the challenges ahead.

I believe in the American Dream. I know it exists because I live it every day as a successful entrepreneur. I provide services and manufacture automated machines in America. I am blessed to have been born in a country where making that vision into a reality is possible, and I don't take it for granted. Sacrates was killed for his requirement to be able to disagree.

But for some time now, the faith in the American Dream seems to be contracting, the entrepreneurial spirit is diminishing and the knowledge of what has allowed for American exceptionalism is no longer being shared. The pessimism that is leading to nihilism about climate, race, politics, and wealth inequality is easy to understand as the negative stories litter our inboxes and news streams. Fear and anger run the algorithms that feed our social media accounts. Meanwhile, humanity's amazing achievements that make life better for billions of people are mostly ignored. I too, have been captured by many of these negative belief systems of scarcity and fear. However, our collective standard of living has never been higher, and our history has shown that we can overcome all the challenges in front of us if we allow entrepreneurs to thrive and develop independent solutions that make our world a better place. We can get past the fear of scarcity, sit in awe at the progress that has already been made, and allow future entrepreneurs to make things even better.

America faces many challenges today, more so than at any other time in my life. What is at stake is not team blue or team red being right or wrong, but the American Dream itself.

My belief that a great future is dependent on entrepreneurs led me to ask some fundamental questions including: how do we get more entrepreneurs? Why are more people are not starting small businesses that will grow and employ others?

More and more I hear anecdotes of students who wanted to be entrepreneurs but were having their dreams stifled, delayed, or outright destroyed because of their financial situation. And that financial situation started with debt, and specifically student loan debt.

This led to more questions about the current education system: why were costs so high? Why so much debt being taken out? And is it possible to get a degree without the massive debt load? Could it be more beneficial to students and families to not pursue a degree?

I was not happy with the results of my research and more importantly, the disservice the current education system is to all students and therefore to entrepreneurs and therefore to the county and the world. The causes are many and can be debated and argued over for decades to come, but the current solution is simple: we need to help students stay out of debt as much as possible!

We need young people to be unencumbered by debt so they can go on to start new businesses, solve the problems we face and live out the American dream. That will make all of our lives better.

I could easily have used the phrase "Our Future Destroyed" for this book because it is all of us who will suffer when entrepreneurs are not allowed to pursue their dreams. We have just lived through a period of great government expansion, where more and more of the economy is being decided by governments instead of by free citizens. Unfortunately, governments are terrible decision makers, because unlike entrepreneurs, they don't have the responsibility of the outcome of their decisions and therefore those decisions are political rather than practical in nature.

Additionally, because of government intervention we have seen the financialization of everything. Allowing the government to control money and interest rates has caused massive distortions. These include the government takeover of student loans, capture of government agencies by corporate interests, money in politics, huge federal deficits, and unfair practices by private equity.

Over the next decade I expect all of this is going to change and we will need more entrepreneurs to make the future better, for the citizens of America, the people of the world as well as the planet. We will need political entrepreneurs to shrink government and reduce its burden on citizens. We will need entrepreneurs in chemistry, physics, and engineering to figure out how to manage plastic waste, clean up the oceans and protect more natural areas. Inventors will figure out how to make energy cheaper and transport it more efficiently. Cheaper energy will make housing more affordable and healthcare more accessible. We will need business entrepreneurs to take over the crumbling assets of failing companies saddled with debt by private equity. We will want and need more small businesses.

Small businesses employ 46.8% of private sector employees. They created 62% of net new jobs since 1995. Most importantly, they give people who work for them access to the owners, so employees are not just a number in a company of thousands, they can know the owner and their ideas for making the world a better place can be heard. It is with the input of everyone that we develop better methods, deploy more efficient technologies, and raise the standard of living for everyone.

This book is intended to help keep the American Dream alive. If it finds only 1 entrepreneur that stays out of student loan debt and gets to fulfill their dreams, then it was worth writing. If it helps families and students not take on more debt than they need and can afford, then it's already a huge success. What I hear most often after discussing these questions with former students is "this would have been really useful before I took out student loans." To all former students, please help share the message with the younger generation and their parents. Please help me create a better future for us all by ensuring the American Dream, and the prosperity it brings to the world, continues.

Many years ago I read *How Will You Measure Your Life* by Clayton Christensen, where he asked that you define your purpose.

At that time (and it still holds true today) I wrote:

To help entrepreneurs create lasting organizations built through teams.

To educate people about freedom and capitalism so they can improve their lives, the lives of their families, their communities and the country.

To be a kind, honest, forgiving and selfless Partner, brother, uncle, son, friend, boss and colleague.

At a recent investment conference one presenter challenged everyone to be a teacher, to help educate others. Many in the crowd wondered how they might do that. I present everyone with the opportunity to help all students and families with the college decision. I don't have the answers, but the questions to be answered and discussed are here for everyone to share and discuss.

Debt is the worst of things when trying to start your adult life and career. While a degree may put you ahead, debt guarantees you start behind. It is a broken system leading many to hold jobs they don't like and have stress they don't need. For those who don't understand the system and end up taking out huge loans, it can be catastrophic to their future. None of us would sign up for a degree that required we give away a huge portion of all of our future earnings. But that is the promise of debt. Student loan debt is ***Special Debt,*** it is one of the few debts that cannot be discharged in bankruptcy and that makes taking on too much debt not just a mistake, but the mistake that can follow you for the rest of your life.

This is a guide to help educate you on the education system and evaluate your options, in the hopes that your college education comes with little or no debt, so you maximize the rewards you receive for your efforts.

Moms out there: This is especially for you! My hope is that this book will help your family make the best education choice for your children. This is one of the biggest choices a family faces and it deserves an informed, thorough process and an understanding of the university system to make the best decision.

Thank you to my best friend, my wife and my rock, Sarah. Without you I would have never finished this book!

Introduction

This is Not Just a Crisis; This is an Epidemic of Destruction (and it's not from COVID-19)

Each year, approximately 3.7 million high school kids receive their high school diplomas. About 67% of those graduates (about 2.5 million) race off to college, all extremely confident they will not only get a degree, but will also land a job they want, at the companies they want, for the salaries they feel they deserve, with a fat benefit package to boot. Then life happens—only 57% (about 1.41 million) of those students who go off to college actually graduate.

Many will find college as boring as high school and will be disappointed with the college curriculum. Some will have family who need their help; others will lack motivation. If that were the entire story, then we would not be calling it a crisis.

Nothing seems wrong or unexpected in the initial enrollment numbers until you analyze the fallout from being a college student - DEBT. About 1 million people with student loans default each year. For the sake of illustration, let's pretend this is a medical scenario. Let's say 2.5 million people will fly on an airplane for the first time this year and one million of them will break their leg at the airport. If that were to happen, what would be the solutions?

We could either educate a lot of doctors and open a treatment center in every airport, or we could get to the root of the problem and stop breaking legs. Unfortunately, we have chosen to do neither and we have a lot of people limping through life burdened by their loans.

Each year, one million more students' default on their loans, and 2.5 million more students go off to college. Rinse and repeat as another 1 million more people cannot repay their loans. And unlike a broken leg that can heal, the 1 million people who can't afford their debts last year, cannot afford them this year either. So, this is a cumulative crisis with more and people impacted by a failed system.

Students Yearly:

- Graduate High School: 3.7 million
- Start College: 2.5 million
- Graduate College: 1.4 million
- Default on their student loans: **1 million**

...ONE MILLION...That is not a typo!

ONE MILLION people default on each year!

Want to know why the economy is not growing and why people can't save for retirement? Beyond monopolies and captured government, it is because the system has set up far too many people to pay for education for their entire lives. It should take no one by surprise that these indebted students are screaming for socialism and government to pay off their debts. Socialism sounds better than being in debt your whole life, even if you give up all your freedoms.

Now, here is the shocking part: This is where it turns into an epidemic and not just a crisis: For the one million people who default on their loans, it is nearly guaranteed that their credit, and their financial future, if not their lives, are destroyed for decades to come, because student loans don't go away. Student loan debt is the worst kind of debt for this reason. If one million people per year defaulted on their credit cards and had to declare bankruptcy, that would be bad. But in bankruptcy, the judge would force the banks to forgive most of those debts based on the person's ability to pay, and they would get a second chance. A chance to start over financially, so that they are not destitute.

> **WHAT WE BELIEVE:**
>
> 94% of parents believe their child will graduate from college
>
> **THE REALITY:**
>
> Only 30% of students will graduate from college

But student loans do not go away, even if the person files bankruptcy, so defaulting on student loans means you are broke, with your credit destroyed, still carrying the debt that you cannot afford to pay. This is why it is ***Special Debt.*** The system does not allow you to start over. Instead, it just ensures your credit will be low and your interest on all other debt high, and debt collectors will hound you for at least a decade. To top it off, they will go after anyone else in your family they can for payments. Typically, these are parents or grandparents who thought they were doing the right thing by co-signing on student loans and are now seeing their paychecks or retirement benefits garnished to make student loan payments for their children or grandchildren.

The worst place to be in life is a place without hope. We are teaching our children a lot of ideas that are not true or helpful, but to burden them financially is different, it's not an idea they can change their mind about, it is a financial reality they have to live with until the debts are repaid.

Debt that you cannot repay is a life without hope. It is a destruction of one's self-worth and a lack of ability to keep one's head above water, much less contribute to society. When there is no clean-slate option, how can these students have hope for a bright financial future, with their credit destroyed and so much debt remaining? That's a deep hole to climb out of for anyone.

We are currently in an EPIDEMIC, and you may be the reason your family gets this disease if you don't wake up to the fact that the system is not set up to help you. You need to know the cost-benefit to your child and for your family.

Carrying student debt makes one less likely to buy home, start a business or save enough for retirement. In short, it adds stress and reduces quality of life. Everyone should be very careful with this decision. Know before you buy!

Do We Expect Children to Make the Right Decisions?

When I started this journey of helping people avoid student loan debt, I thought that my audience was 18-year-old students headed off to college. But the more I talked to them, the more I realized how idealistic I was at 18 and why no one will ever put someone with a brain that is not fully formed in charge of crucial things, like a business. But for some reason we have given these children the decision to take on life changing amounts of debt. It is not that children are not capable of making decisions; it is that they are too young and inexperienced to truly understand the consequences of their choices. When it comes to college, there are so many factors involved, it became impossible for me to separate them to deliver a clear message that has a chance of getting through to the youth of today. So, I wrote this as a guide for parents, to help you to sit down with your children and make the best decision for your family.

The student loan crisis starts with the cultural aspect of college expectations. According to Pew Research, 94% of parents think their child is going to college (presumably, not just attend but also graduate with a degree). However, only about 30% of children will actually graduate. Obviously, our culture has done a great job of making everyone believe this is the common, necessary track for all, and thus, parents ignore reality that only a third actually cross the finish line, meanwhile almost all rack up debt in the process.

Then we have to consider the competitive nature of college, students and parents, many of which are caught up in the idea that where you go to school indicates how smart you are, or how good of a parent you were—none of which makes sense. Not everyone is engaged and does well in school, especially high school, and not everyone who gets into an Ivy League school will do great things in life. Who you become as a person is essential; where you go to school is much less important than what you do once you are on campus and what you do once you leave campus.

But school rankings, test preparation, and well-funded marketing campaigns by universities keep everyone believing that where they attend school is of paramount importance. Competition between classmates over admissions into higher ranked schools is rampant. How it all gets paid for, and the impact of debt is often an afterthought or not discussed at all.

Meanwhile, the statistics tell a different story—in many cases, the value proposition no longer makes sense. But try convincing any 18-year old that facts matter. No one can understand the burden of debt until you have to live with it.

As a business owner I've lived with debt for most of my adult life, so I understand debt and its potential consequences. Some debt for equipment that can be used to make things or provide services can be very good for a business or a household. Too much debt and quickly you are no longer the owner and most or all of your earnings could be needed to pay interest. Worst case: I could lose all the assets of the business and the bank sells them. Worst case: I'm bankrupt and back to zero.

While that is awful, it is not forever, it is not ***Special Debt***. The burden of ***Special Debt*** is different, it is for forever, it is a potential mistake for which there may be no forgiveness. This is not fair and should be changed. But until then, it is up to each of us to know the rules and make the best decisions and avoiding as much Special Debt as you can is a good rule of thumb.

Conventional wisdom dictates that you have to take out debt to go to university unless your parents are wealthy—it is just part of what you have to do, according to the "experts". And the "experts" have likely made you and every other student believe that debt is a requirement to go to college unless the family has saved enough money, which seems impossible given the massive increases in tuition versus average salaries. I heard it from my 16-year-old niece last Christmas without any supporting arguments, like "it's just common knowledge", and the attitude that came with it said that I was an idiot to think otherwise. They want you to keep thinking that debt is inevitable because it supports an otherwise unsupportable system. The government created this disaster, and they are not going to save you from it, so you can keep believing what they tell you, or do your own research and make informed decisions.

Most importantly, parents are scared. They're scared that by not supporting their child going to college, whatever the cost, their child will end up with a lower standard of living. Ironically, it is this type of thinking that will *guarantee* the lower standard of living, because while a degree carries some value, the total cost of debt can be astronomical, and the repayment likely wasn't correctly calculated when signing for the loans. What was measured instead was only family pride and prestige. **The truth is the way to ensure your child falls out or never rises to the middle class is to allow them to take on tens or hundreds of thousands of dollars in debt.** They may end up with middle class earnings, but their debt can sink them into a lower class lifestyle.

PATH TO PROSPERITY:

- You work for your benefit.
- Debt is only used for major purchases like:
  -Home
  -Car
  -Business
- Interest expense is minimized.

PATH TO POOR:

- Debt is used for everything and interest

As I mentioned earlier, this is also not "normal" debt, it is ***Special Debt***. This is the type of debt that is never treated as a mistake in decision-making and cannot be discharged in bankruptcy. It's debt that lasts forever and may even end up costing you part of your retirement or may ensure your new graduate is too broke to live on their own and has to live in your basement for another decade. Or two. Why go off to college and spend all the money on housing to move back home? Is the college experience worth that?

For many young people, student loan debt is their first introduction to any debt transaction and for most students it is the first decision of real consequence. That we allow such choices, with such severe consequences to be made with so little understanding is a large part of my reason for writing this book.

In order to end this epidemic, parents need to have real talks with their kids. We certainly can't leave it up to the students themselves to end this crisis, because they lack the wisdom to understand the consequences of their decision making, and they are being fueled by a collective ~~dream~~ delusion. They have been sold the dream of a college lifestyle of freedom and exploration is priceless and that they should pursue this at any price. It is your responsibility as a parent to sit them down and engage in the hard discussions about budgets, costs and the lifelong impact of debt and specifically ***Special Debt***. Of course, there are several cases where the student's level of ambition and proposed degree are actually a good value proposition. In this case, I say go for it! But stop your child from majoring in art history and thinking they're going to land a six-figure entry level salary. The truth is they ~~might not~~ will probably not even use their specific major in the real world.

If the statistics for an infectious disease or broken limbs were the same as the student loan statistics, we would shut down the entire system, just like they did for COVID-19. You wouldn't allow your child to leave the house and go to college; you'd be worried for their safety. The reality is, you should be worried for their safety, their financial safety and their mental well-being, neither or which do well under stress from debt. Don't allow your child's college decision to destroy their financial future. Or yours!

A Note About How to Use This Book:

To make better decisions, we need to analyze the entire college decision, consider its value, the cost, and the long-term consequences of debt. This guide is meant to ask all the questions and understand the ramifications of those decisions long term.

I recommend that students and parents go through this process separately at first, and then together. Take time to answer these questions separately and then discuss them together. This will help to show differences in expectations and opinions of each party and allow for further in-depth discussions.

This guide will not provide you with easy answers. The right answers are going to be different for each person, but this will guide you through all the information you should consider in making an informed decision. It will also show you a path to graduating without debt if you're willing to put in the work before and during college.

I designed the program this book offers to teach you about this rigged game so you can try to play it to the best of your ability. I want you to get your degree if that is your path, understand the true value that a degree carries, and then decide how much of your future earnings you are willing to give up for it. Along the journey you will learn ways to pay the least amount to get the same degree. Instead of paying Maserati prices for a Honda Accord degree, you'll pay Honda prices.

Don't get fixated on any particular number, most data points can individually be argued, it is the process that matter. Future estimates of value and inflation are educated guesses. The total benefits of a degree will depend on what degree you get and what it costs you versus your additional earnings. Figure out your specifics. Develop **YOUR** plan.

In the space provided in each chapter, write down your first thoughts for each question. This is not a test; it is a place for you to explore options and learn. In the final chapter, there is space for you to go back through each question and compile your thoughts to create your plan.

PART 1

Good Intentions on the Hero's Journey

Let's start with a tale of higher learning: its hopes, fulfillment of dreams, and associated costs...

Mary always had a smile on her face when her parents told her they were proud of her. Like most children, she wanted her parents' approval, and school was the area where she felt their support the most, and so she put tremendous effort into studying and getting good grades. Her parents were both college graduates, and from the time she was a small child, her attending college was a foregone conclusion.

Mary had to study more than some of her friends, but she didn't mind. She got good grades, took AP classes, and studied hard and took prep classes for the ACT and SAT. She wanted to make her parents proud by getting into the highest ranked school that she could. Ultimately, she excelled, got into many of the schools she applied to and went about getting her degree.

During her childhood, Mary's parents had some medical problems and were not able to save as much as they would have preferred for her education. Their income was just high enough so that Mary could not receive government grants. She did receive a few scholarships, and all the schools she visited made it very clear that she could get all the "financial aid" she needed in the form of loans. Mary graduated with a degree in communications and $80K of student loan debt. Mary's parents were very proud at graduation, and she felt good about her accomplishments. It was only later that she would realize the burden of her student loan debt.

After the six months of automatic deferrals, her first bill came, almost $700 per month. Mary's salary was $40K per year, and she also had health benefits, so it seemed like she was off to a good start. But with the hefty student loan payment, Mary struggled to pay all of her bills, even with roommates. She used credit cards to cover the difference and to have some fun on the weekends. After all, she deserved it after spending the last four years studying and working hard in school.

Mary wanted to have a family but soon realized the cost of having a child was not affordable to her at the time. Most of the men she met also had large amounts of student loan debt and struggled to make ends meet. At 28, Mary had her first major setback, the company she worked for had not received the additional funding they needed, and almost all the staff were laid off. While the unemployment money helped, it was not enough to cover the bills and Mary fell deeper into credit card debt as she looked for another job. The new job she accepted was for less money than she was previously making but was better than no job at all.

Entering her 30's, Mary began to really feel the stress of her debt. Her student loan debt was shrinking, but not very fast. Meanwhile, her credit card debt was increasing, and Mary had saved very little for retirement and had nothing in savings. She wanted to have more experiences with her friends, but she had to charge everything on credit cards, which she knew was unwise. She was close to using all her income just to make minimum credit card and student loan payments and to cover her monthly bills. She had worked so hard and felt she had nothing to show for it.

The depression didn't start all at once, it crept up more slowly, beginning as a bit of sadness and slowly becoming a feeling of despair. Every day she felt as though she was trapped, working for someone else with all her money going to others. She had nothing left for herself, and she felt ashamed, as though she had done something wrong when she had done exactly what everyone in her life had told her to do.

She was angry, but that anger had no focal point. Where should it be targeted? It made no sense; she had done precisely what everyone said she was supposed to do in order to succeed and live a good life. Mary's depression eventually led to additional health problems, and she was frequently at her doctor's office. Her health was on a downward spiral, both physically and mentally, and she didn't know what to do. Her doctor told her she needed to reduce her stress. Meanwhile, the doctor bills and cost of prescriptions were adding to her anxiety, creating a horrible cycle of debt, causing stress that was leading to disease that was causing more debt that was causing more stress...

The Debt Impact on Your Life

Talk to recent college graduates or read their stories, and most of them will tell you about how they are suffering from way too much debt. There seems to be a new article about student loan debt written every day, like a recent NY Times article from March 18, 2021 where Molly Webster outlines how she graduated with $78,000 of debt, has made payments of $60,000 and still owes more than $100,000. Unfortunately, this story is not unique.

Student loan debt is most aptly described as an albatross born of aspiration. Debt is a promise of your future earnings and can best be thought of as bricks in a backpack that you must carry around. Let's say one brick = $1,000 of debt. A few bricks are not a real problem. If you're financially strong (leaving college with the promise of a larger entry-level salary), you might be able to carry a few more bricks, but eventually, no matter how strong you are, if you put enough bricks in the backpack, you won't be able to carry it at all. It will keep you in place or drown you.

If you are required to carry a lot of bricks for a long time, it will have adverse effects on your body. We can view this as a physical strain – bricks in a backpack that you can't put down will cause lower back pain, shoulder pain, and will feel heavier over time. But what about the psychological impacts of the bricks and the backpack you can't put down? How long will it take before you are mentally exhausted from all the pain of carrying the bricks? At which point are you so worn down physically and mentally that you want to give up?

These are the unseen burdens of debt, and student loan debt, being ***Special Debt*** is one of the worst kinds. You can't get rid of it! This is where the government has truly failed its citizens. If student loan debt cannot be discharged in bankruptcy, then there should be a lot of education and controls around it. Instead, debt is sold by universities as "aid". Tuition keeps on rising, in large part because debt is readily available. As long as students continue to pay the higher tuition and take on the debt, the process will likely continue, as our dysfunctional government is unlikely to fix anything. Most government solutions end up causing more problems regardless of their original intent. This student loan crisis began as the government's "solution" so everyone could have an opportunity at getting a university degree. It has turned into a crisis.

This does not mean that no one should attend college; it means that we need to have a new collective awareness around debt, that we need to educate young people on the lifelong impacts of debt, especially ***Special Debt***. Debt leads to stress, which leads to disease. If we view debt in this more holistic way, it's easy to see there's more value in reducing one's debt from education, than in making the family proud because of the university name on the diploma.

Not All Debt is the Same

While the principle that debt is a burden and may be taking away more of your future than you bargained for, sometimes, in the right situations, debt can be a useful tool. This is not the debt from living on campus, refusing to have a job while in school, or going to the most expensive institution. The "good" kind of debt is debt that gets you to making more money faster. If you are an intelligent student who understands the cost of education, knows what kind of job that you want, and has a realistic expectation of your future wages, then taking on some debt to finish school sooner may be a good idea.

> **WHAT IS DEBT?**
>
> **DEFINITION:**
>
> » *Something owed*
> » *An obligation to pay*
> » *A promise of your future earnings*

As a thought exercise, if you could expect to earn a $60,000 salary after an investment in yourself, versus $40,000 if you did not make then investment, then the benefit of the investment is easy to measure, at $20,000. As I will show you, that increase in salary does not amount to an additional $20,000 per year as the simple math would like to show you (remember taxes), but the benefit is still significant— around $14,000 per year, net of taxes.

The question you need to ask is, what amount of investment, and in this case debt, are you willing to take on to get to that extra $14k per year of net earnings sooner?

Let us assume that you will need to borrow an additional $10,000 to go to summer school so you can graduate one semester earlier than you would otherwise. That extra $10,000 you have to spend will be earned by you in about 9 months of additional salary and that would allow you to repay the loan and interest quickly. But what if you had to borrow an additional $30,000 and that would take you closer to 3 years or more of work to pay off this debt? The first situation sounds reasonable, but the second situation looks like too much additional debt for the benefit of early graduation, just based on time. But what if you could graduate one year early instead of one semester? Or what if you only needed an additional $5,000 of debt to graduate early? These are great thought experiments.

Your situation is unique to you, but sometimes, students forego graduating early in an effort to eliminate all debts. If you must borrow $5,000 to graduate a semester early, which allows you to earn an additional $7,000 with your degree in a short time frame, then that is a good trade off. Take on the debt and pay it back immediately with the additional earnings. The second potential upside to this situation is that you are on the job earlier, which means your real-world education starts sooner and the value you bring to an organization can start rising sooner.

The point of this exercise is to show that not all debt is bad if it can lead to getting a degree faster, which leads to you making more money sooner. It is impossible to show all the potential financial outcomes for your education, but part of the process can include some debt if it makes sense. Only you can decide that, but when you do this analysis, make sure you have realistic expectations for your future salary and the likelihood of receiving that job before committing to more debt. Too many students sign up for the debt with unrealistic expectations of their salary after school.

More debt is rarely a good thing, but in specific circumstances, not taking on small amounts of debt that can be repaid quickly can result in a loss of earnings. Overall, completing these thought exercises about short term and long term debt decisions can help you make a more informed decision on how much of your future earnings you are giving up for a degree.

Education is Broken

The entire primary education system is now designed to prepare everyone for college, but ***only 33% of students who start high school will get a college degree.***

What about the other 66% of students?

The College Mobility Illusion

Despite the fact that most of us will not end up with the "prestigious" jobs that the Ivy League promises, college, or some technical training after high school, is often necessary, if not for upward mobility then just not to drop lower in income level and lifestyle. In the early 1900s, less than 10% of students graduated from high school because there were plenty of labor jobs that didn't require an education. As the world changed, so did the skill requirements, and a high school diploma became a prerequisite for a career in the middle class. The world has since changed, and the technology revolution now requires more skills to keep that middle-class job.

On the one hand, we are forced to accept the fact that the grand social mobility we have been sold is a lie, and on the other hand, we know that many middle-class jobs now require a college degree or other formal education. But the cost of this degree can be more than the future earnings benefit, especially if you come from a lower-income family.

Economists Timothy Bartik and Brad Hershbein, in their paper "*Degrees of Poverty, The Relationship Between Family Income Background and the Return to Education,*" show the statistics of how a college degree affects future earnings and the relationship to family earnings. More detailed than the Pew research that gives an overall average of about $600,000 of additional lifetime earnings for those who have a degree, the research of Bartik and Hershbein shows that a degree will increase earnings more for higher-income families than lower-income families. If you grow up in a lower-income family, your bachelor's degree benefit is only $335,000 over your lifetime. Students from higher-income families see a disproportionate share of the benefits, and the wealthy see the most substantial benefits as described above.

Part of this difference makes sense in the system of capitalism. Those who have more capital in their family today will benefit more in the future from additional education, allowing them to deploy the family's wealth to earn even more. If you start with no capital, or worse, large amounts of debt, how are you ever going to participate in capitalism?

What all the research seems to indicate is that the major benefits of college are going to those who don't just have a bachelor's degree, but advanced degrees in science, business, and medicine. What is always difficult to extract from the data is how much support these graduate students receive from their families. It is easy to understand how there are greater earnings for advanced degrees, especially in science, medicine and

4.4 Million	U.S. Students who start high school annually
704,000	The roughly 16% who drop out before graduation
2.5 Million	Of those who graduate high school, 67% of those go to college (but remember, 16% don’t make it through high school)
1.4 Million	Only 57% of those who start college actually graduate with a degree
33% Students	**Total number of students who graduate BOTH high school and college**

engineering.

The very first podcast that I did on student loan debt is titled "Understanding How the Student Loan System is Set Up Against

You." I stand by that statement, and all additional research continues to inform me that the entire education system needs an overhaul. If only 40% of high school graduates go on to get a bachelor's degree, and 16% of high school students drop out, **we are spending almost all of our primary education resources on the 33% who will graduate from college** (see chart below).

Still, the vast majority of gains go to the elite, who have their own system to keep the Ivy League system working for them.

I can't fix all the mess of the education system, and neither can you, that is a Big Ask. We would need to overhaul how we tax the wealthy and their estates to eliminate the elite class and legacies of the same families (good luck—the Rockefellers and Kennedys don't share this opinion). We would need to overhaul the entire education system to offer alternative pathways for students who want to study a trade and find new channels to teach the job skills required for students who are not going to college. And then, we would need to overhaul the college system, eliminate sports as a business (or at least pay the athletes), and get rid of all the administrators to reduce costs, and instead focus education on the transfer of information for the betterment of society at the lowest cost to its citizens. I'm not sure about you, but that's a fight I'm not taking on.

All we can do is acknowledge the value proposition we have and make the most of it. The worst case is that you go to college, drop out, and have a lot of debt you have to repay with few skills and no degree. Also terrible is a degree with a lot of debt like our friend Mary.

A degree no longer guarantees you upward mobility, but many trades pay well and only require a certificate, Associate degree or even no degree at all. Still, a college education can help many students, and society has deemed it the new prerequisite for many middle-class jobs. But if you reduce the benefit of having a degree by taking on large amounts of debt, then your life will be even worse: You'll be an indentured servant, living in stress, until you die.

The intelligent path forward, as an individual and a family, is to learn the game and make better choices.

***

Your first college course is this one – a course on college and the burden of debt.

We have discussed the general societal expectations where most parents think their kids are going to college when the facts show only 33% of them will graduate. What other questions should we be asking? Here is a starter list, but add your own questions for your consideration on why you hold certain beliefs about the value of a university degree and where you should go:

Questions for prospective students:

Do you feel as though your parents would do **anything** for you?

____

____

____

____

____

Do you feel pressure to reach a level of academic achievement? Is this family pressure, peer pressure, personal pressure or a mix?

Does it feel like a college degree is more important to your family than to you?

Do you feel pressure from your friends on where to attend school?

Do you believe universities have created an image for you of what the college experience will be?

At what age were you first told you were going to go to college? Who told you?

At what age does the mind finish developing? (hint: Google it!)

Do you believe the same things that are important to you now will be important to you when you are 30? List the five most important things to you right now.

Is there a specific school you want to attend? Will you be disappointed if you don't get in?

Does your family have discussions about finance, tuition costs, and the value of a university degree?

Questions for parents:

Does it matter to you if your child attends college? Why or why not?

Does it matter to you where your child attends college? If so, why?

What are your hopes and dreams for your child's career path, if any?

Where do you see your child in five, ten, or twenty years? Do you believe they see themselves in that same situation?

Why I Got Involved

Student loan debt was not a subject of great passion for me. I'm a small business owner, and my specialty is small business, finance, and taxes. I love helping small business owners. From conceptual ideas through selling the business, it amazing to watch ideas become companies and change to become reality.

When I was in college, I thought I wanted to be a professor and to teach on a college campus. I love teaching and helping others. A wise friend and I discussed my desire to help others, and he advised me that pursuing a teaching job at a university would be the worst thing for me.

He told me I had real-world knowledge, and practical knowledge is not something that the academic community embraces with open arms. He said I would be frustrated by the bureaucracy of the institutions. The more research I did and the more people I talked with confirmed this wise man's theory and advice. Over the years, I have come up with many ways to transfer knowledge and pass along what I have learned. It wasn't until hearing the story of a specific family I know that I decided to take a more in-depth look into the student loan crisis. Through my research I realized what a mess it was and how it was negatively affecting students and families' futures, en masse.

Worse, it is preventing future business owners from living out their vision for the future. It is killing the American Dream. That was my call to take action.

This is a short version of that story, with names and places changed to protect identities.

Elise loves animals and worked at a veterinarian's office during high school. Working with animals confirmed for Elise that she wanted to spend her life helping animals and their owners. As she neared her senior year of high school, she began looking at different schools to fulfill her dream. She felt she found the perfect place to study when she and her parents visited Colorado State University.

Colorado State University staff warmly greeted Elise and her family and told her all about their outstanding veterinarian program. The university let her know that to complete that degree, she would need first to complete her bachelor's degree, then she would need to apply to the graduate degree program, and both programs would each take four years. They also informed her that most states would require her to complete a residency program before she could be issued a veterinary license. The staff reiterated that attending Colorado State for the undergraduate degree would vastly improve the chances of Elise being accepted into the veterinarian program.

Elise had a dream, and now it had a timetable— eight years and then work for someone else for a couple of years, and then she could be licensed. Her parents were excited for her and were proud of her decision to pursue that path. Though the family was not well off, they imagined Elise's accomplishment of going to school and being a vet would bring great pride to the family.

The family was encouraged by the university not to waste any time and to enroll the following year. The university sent over the financial "aid" package that listed the costs of tuition and room and board, the scholarship she would be receiving, and the student loans available to cover any additional amounts the family could not afford to pay out of pocket. It was, of course, required that Elise live on campus the first year.

Because Elise was coming from Minnesota, she would have to pay out-of-state tuition, but the scholarship covered half of that amount. While she was a good student, Elise wasn't a valedictorian or at the top of her class, so she didn't qualify for too any additional scholarships. The family made just enough money that Elise didn't qualify for federal grants.

No one ever sat down with family and reviewed what loans for eight years of school would look like or that the total debt for Elise when she graduated would be over $250,000. Nor did anyone sit down and explain what that monthly payment would look like after college. To an 18-year-old with a dream, it was just money, and whatever forms they put in front of her, she signed in order to be closer to reaching that dream. And who wouldn't want to support these dreams?

But what are the job prospects after college? How much does Elise's salary need to be to pay down all these loans comfortably? None of these things were discussed. No one investigated how much veterinarians make or discussed how this would translate into being able to repay all of the "financial aid" that magically turns into debt upon graduation.

Before hearing about Elise, I happened to read an article about how poorly veterinarians are being paid, and how a few large firms are buying up all the small offices, paying vets less and less. Because of their debt, fewer and fewer are able to open their own businesses, even though that is what most of them thought would eventually happen.

This story literally brought me to tears. I could see beyond the veil of the story to the financial difficulty that lay in store for Elise, where the dream slowly dies because no one was looking out for her in the long-term. The university has enrollment to fill; the bank, loans to make, and both see Elise, not as a person with a dream, but someone to help them make their numbers.

I'm not saying that no one at Colorado State University cares, I'm sure there are many professors who are loved by their students. What I will say is that the incentives are not in place to do what is best for the student.

As of this writing, a veterinarian's mean salary is $88,000 per year. For the next 20 years, Elise will have a monthly student loan payment of over $2,000. This means that of her lifetime earnings, **she will have to make over $700,000 to pay for her education.** Did anyone give her this actual figure when she signed up for the loan? Of course not.

That's not a good value for anyone except the university and the banks, so things need to change, and the long-term interests of students and their families need to come first. In no free market society would anyone loan a child (and if you're 18, you're still a child physically as your brain is still developing) $250,000 for a job with a mean salary of $88,000 per year.

It was Elise's story that made me decide to write this book. To hear about the dream of a future entrepreneur, who wanted to open her own place and help animals and see the future would not allow it, it crushed me. It began the questions of why, when and WTF? The more research I did, the more disturbed I became by the entire system.

The money game of college has changed. In the 20 years since I left college, costs have risen by up to 500%. Why? There's really no good reason. Professors are not being paid 500% more, inflation has not been 500%, job are not paying 500% more and there are fewer tenured professors (those with true academic freedom). Students, who are merely following the advice they've been told their whole lives, counseled by the schools to take on debt disguised as *financial aid*, are getting the worst end of the deal. Once I started looking deeper, the stories of students saddled with debt seemed to come almost daily. But everyone acted like this debt was inevitable, that it was the only way to get a degree. I did more research, and I can tell you that the inevitability of debt for a degree is not valid, and I'm going to share that research with you.

The entire system is a frustrating mess, and in the Supplement section I add in the research on how we got to this crisis if you're interested. Some of the causes are from good intentions but no one is saying, "enough is enough." While caused by the government, the rest of this crisis is a crisis of misinformation and poor decision making. You have the choice to decide to take on debt, and you also have the option to say no to debt. You can still get the degree you want—I'll show you ways to do it—but freedom has a price. The price of financial freedom means you will have to work for it, but it is possible to get the degree you want, from a great institution, without the massive burden of debt that could last a lifetime.

MYTH:

Debt is required to get a degree unless your parents can afford to pay for school.

This is a narrative to keep schools full when regardless of whether they deliver the future value

These debts have consequences; none of them good. As debt levels rise opportunities reduce. More debt leads to fewer entrepreneurs, fewer homeowners, fewer parents, less of all the things people want. Less of the things that create more prosperity for all of us. That needs to change!

PART 2

The 'Why' of College

Question 1:

Why do you believe a college education is right for you? (Typical answers: to have the college experience, increase job opportunities, explore interests, learn about the world, get a good job, make more money in life, etc.)

____

____

____

____

____

____

____

Do you know what job you want after school?

____

____

____

____

____

Question 2:

What do you hope the degree you are seeking will bring you and your family? (Typical answers: intelligence, wealth, status, happiness, better job).

The 'Why' Explored

Did anyone write down an answer for Q2 of: *I want to be in debt so I can give my earnings to someone else my whole life?* I didn't think so, but that is more and more often the case. The fact that **the cost of a 4-year degree has risen 550% over the past 20 years** shows us that unfortunately, students are working more to pay off their debts than they are to build wealth or improve their standard of living. Members of my family are still paying off their student loans 20 years after graduation. It is getting worse every year as costs continue to rise.

College is an interesting part of American and other advanced economic cultures. Founded initially on hard sciences and the quest for truth about the world around us, universities now more resemble political institutions of ideas instead of teaching scientific and Socratic methods that allow us to continue to learn about the world around us.

The necessity of a bachelor's degree is now a foregone conclusion in the public consciousness, valued more than the pursuit of training and knowledge acquired elsewhere. Apprenticeships no longer seem valuable despite the need for them in the workplace. While science is still the reason universities continue to exist, most students do not graduate with degrees in hard sciences, and many of the jobs they obtain after school don't even require a college degree.

The statistics show how much the idea of college is indoctrinated into our societal norms. As we've already discussed, while almost all parents believe their kids will go to college, only 1/3 of starting high school students actually graduate from college. Meanwhile, our whole education system centers on and pushes everyone to the college track. This obviously doesn't make any sense.

Parents are understandably optimistic about their children, and everyone wants to believe their child is exceptional. What's happening is that almost all of our educational resources for high school education are going to the 1/3 of students who will get a 4-year degree. What about the other two-thirds of students? That is, the two out of every three who are in programs that will not really benefit them? This is part of the reason for the high dropout rate of high school students. **High school students usually don't have other curriculum options that will actually benefit them, so why not work more hours at a job at 17?** A lot of students do. So why not you? Because you probably believe the common narrative: a college degree is necessary to *get ahead*, or at the very least not fall behind. Meanwhile, with all the debt required to get that degree, everyone ~~seems to be~~ is falling further behind.

> **MYTH:**
>
> College will teach you what you need to know.
>
> The truth is that your education should never end and there are more things they cannot teach you in school then things they can.

The data show us that our system is not serving most students. This doesn't mean we shouldn't have programs for college-bound students, we certainly should. But we should also have other paths to teach skills such as carpentry, plumbing, electrical, and other trades. These programs could easily be combined with employers to offer internships and apprenticeships for all of the jobs that we continue to need, but no one seems to want to do, because we are all told that everyone should go to college. We can and should do better to serve the two-third of students who will not get a 4-year degree, and before we ask the government to take over college, let's make them fix high school education first to prove they can. But I digress...let's save that argument for another time.

The next common misperception is that college will teach you what you need to know to thrive in the world. However, in practice, education is not “one and done”, where a single institution has all of the answers to how the world works. Learning is a lifelong process. You need to *learn how to learn*, not simply be taught what someone else thinks you should know. Hopefully, the college experience will teach you how to be responsible (show up on time for classes and exams, meet deadlines for papers and projects, etc.) and work with others in groups to accomplish projects—valuable skills for the “real world”.

One of the things that colleges don't like to discuss is how much they cannot actually teach you. Let's take business, for example. You can get a degree in business (which I did), and a business school will teach you some aspects of business such as accounting, marketing, finance, and management, but what is business? Business isn't a single skill that you can test to determine if I know it or not. "Business" is an all-encompassing term that is a composite of both knowledge and skills. It could be

the creation of, or selling of a product or service, and also could be dealing with business partners; overseeing operations; evaluating systems and efficiencies; hiring, managing and firing employees; working with regulatory agencies, shareholders, lawyers,
accountants, etc.

It also includes networking, hiring, mentoring, developing people, developing and adapting products and processes, finding or creating markets, and many other skills. They can't teach you these things in college, and it is highly unlikely administrators will know or discuss the limits of the education for which you are paying.

MYTH:

Business is a teachable skill.

The truth is that business is not a skill, it is an all-encompassing term and some aspects of business they can teach you.

An easy example: when should you fire someone?

There should be a course in business schools about the limits of what they teach you, so students stop entering the workforce thinking what they've been taught has high value. The value is your ability to continue to learn, adapt and think critically.

When I graduated with degrees in accounting and management as well as an MBA, I thought I knew a lot, and I felt ready to contribute immediately in my new accounting job. In reality, what I had learned in college was mostly vocabulary. I could speak business words, I knew a little theory, and I understood the vocabulary. But I had no useful skills that I brought to the workplace. They had to teach me everything practical about the job.

The first tax return project I received I completed and handed in to one of the partners. The next day the partner brought the folder to my desk and asked, “Where are the workpapers?” I replied, “Oh, sorry, I’ll add them and get this back to you.” As the partner walked away, I turned to a colleague sitting next to me to ask, “What are workpapers?” In a single moment it was crystal clear how little I knew.

Recently I caught up with a friend who went back to school to complete an MBA at around 30. I asked her, "Do you think you learned more in the two years getting your MBA or in the six years since"? Her reply was, "I can't even remember what I learned in school, but I've been doing nothing but learning since." As for the $100,000 she borrowed getting her MBA, she said that while able to pay those loans off because of her increased salary, she wished we would have had more conversations about ways she could have reduced that amount before signing up for it. Similar stories abound, but the more unfortunate stories are from those like Elise and Mary with the debt similar to my friend, but without the significant increase in earnings to pay it off.

The college experience is often our cultural transition into adulthood. For most students, it is the first time they will live on their own and begin to learn the requirements for an independent life. They get to meet new friends, hopefully get exposed to different cultures, ideas, and areas of interest. However, since college costs have risen over 500% in the past 20 years, this is no longer an experience we can legitimately view as one that is great for "growing up."

> **SELDOM MENTIONED**
>
> 20% of college graduates would be better off if they had not gone to college... because debt ruins lives.
>
> How many more lives are ruined when students don't get a degree?

Parents need to realize that there can be severe, lifelong consequences for pushing their children into what they believe is going to be the same college experience they had years ago. There is a higher likelihood they could end up like Mary, drowning in debt and depression.

The cost of the college experience is no longer unconditionally "worth it," especially if that cost means signing up for huge amounts of debt. In fact, it could just as easily be argued that staying at home and going to community college could be better for the student. If we recall the case for Mary, which is not uncommon today and is shown by the **$1.5 trillion in student loan debt**, the debt is becoming a long-term burden that may not be worth it. It's at least a discussion you need to have before signing up for student loan debt.

According to a recent *Economist* article on education in Britain, the Institute for Fiscal Studies has calculated that a fifth, or 20%, of graduates, would be better off if they had never gone to university. Four in 10 students in the US still do not graduate within six years after starting their degree and for those that do, the wage premium is shrinking.

What a lot of students continue to believe is the idea that their education, especially at smaller private liberal arts schools, is *priceless*. This is a term I highly recommend that no one uses because there is indeed a price that you pay, and when you are drowning in debt from a *priceless* experience, I'm sure your future self, still paying off student loans in your 50's will completely disagree. Let's face it: When we are young our optimism is almost unlimited, while our perspective is very limited, and we need our parents and community to help us make better decisions to protect our future self, especially from debt. Unfortunately, too many "experts" continue to push this narrative. No college experience is *priceless,* precisely because, by definition, *there is a price you pay* to obtain it.

What if you were offered a job for $1,000,000 dollars or more per year, to leave college. Would you take it? You say this is impossible, but Zion Williamson did exactly that: he left Duke to go to the NBA and make millions. If college were *priceless*, Zion would have stayed in school, but school is not priceless, even at an elite university like Duke. Further, if the degree was *priceless*, then you have to explain why many of the most successful people in the world left college?

How do you walk away from *priceless?* You don't, but you do walk towards the best decision for your family, and that is why the use of this word should be limited. But let's transition this argument to what the value of a degree is really worth to you.

From a strictly financial perspective, the data says that on average, college graduates will make an additional $550,000 over a 40-year work life (Pew Research: Is College Worth It, p. 83). Assuming this is the case for our friend Mary, she will have to earn approximately $230,000 to pay for her student loan debt.

(We'll get into this later; debt worksheets are in the back of the book to calculate these real costs). This equation includes money earned, taxes paid, interest paid, and principal paid. So almost half of the benefit Mary will receive for getting her 4-year degree will go to someone other than Mary! The majority of that money will go to the university, and another large chunk will go to big banks. Yeah, those same big banks everyone hates unless they work there!

QUESTION:

How much of your future earnings are you willing to give away to a school for a degree?

Let's go back to our earlier questions and explore some of the standard answers to Question 2: *What do you hope the degree you are seeking will bring you and your family?*

If you answered this question with "more lifetime earnings," you could see from Mary's experience that you are giving away most of that benefit to the school you attend and big banks if you swallow the current sales pitch and sign up for lots of debt. Another standard answer to this question is "for family prestige." This is often the number one real answer for parents, especially East Coast parents. Parents sending their kids off to college feel like they have done their job well and are better parents than those whose kids are not going off to college. Moreover, many parents believe that the higher ranking the school, the equally "higher-ranking" they are as a parent. We will discuss the school rankings in detail in Part 4, but please don't be a parent who cares about rankings. Ranking is a zero-sum game. There can only be one person ranked on top, and for you to move up, someone else needs to step down. If you win at this game and are on top, everyone hates you and wants to take your spot. This is not how life works.

We are here to help each other, not to rank ourselves better than others. They don't have better books at higher-ranked schools, and they may have more famous professors, but that doesn't mean they are better teachers or that school is the right place for your child to study.

If Mary went to the highest-ranked school she could get into but took out even more debt to do it, how will Mary's parents feel years later when Mary is depressed and burdened with these cumbersome student loan bills?

Would you be a better parent if your child had no debt, became a plumbing apprentice, and ended up making $100,000 a year without student loans to pay off? Would that make you a worse parent? What if that was a job your child enjoyed? Let's not lose sight of what is essential: that children have the opportunity to pursue their own ambitions and become their best self. As a parent, it's your duty to be honest with them about the amount of money the family is going to spend on college and the burden of debt. If learning new things is the objective, the library is full of free books, the same books the priceless universities sell you.

In the movie Good Will Hunting, Matt Damon's character, retorting to a Harvard student who was regurgitating what he read as though it was his own idea said, "The sad thing about a guy like you is that in 50 years you are going to start doing some thinking on your own, and will come up with two certainties –

one, don't do that – and two, you dropped $150,000 on an education you coulda got for $1.50 in late fees at the public library." The point here is that learning is available all day, every day at your local library. Today, there are even more opportunities through platforms like MasterClass, YouTube, or Skillshare, and the library is still a great option.

The hard part of this discussion about college and debt is that there is no right answer. We are all different, we have different ambitions and dreams, and value different things. As such, I can't offer you the right or wrong answer, **but let's have a long conversation and ask some important questions** and examine college for what it is and what it's worth so you can make the best decision for your family.

Takeaways on 'Why'

» The current cost of college means we must analyze it differently. This massive increase in financial burden and the long-term stress that debt can create means we need to examine the desire to have the "college experience" differently than we did in the past.

» College is not an end to education, and a campus is not the only place to learn. There are a lot of things— in fact, the majority of things— that school cannot teach you. As mentioned, they cannot teach you "business," as it is not a definable skill. They can only teach you some aspects of business.

» Education is a lifelong endeavor, and you will learn a lot more after school than while in it.

» The cost of school needs to be weighed against the benefits, and we need to include the stress that comes with debt as part of the price. The college experience has a value, but that value must be weighed against the burden of debt.

Don't Forget the 'What'

One of my friends teaches in the community college system in the state of California. One of the issues she raised with me after reading a draft of this book was how many students think they know which job they want, but don't fully understand the degree requirements for that job. I can relate to that as I too was an ignorant young adult. When I started school as an accounting major, I had no idea that just to sit to take the CPA exam required over 150 college credit hours. That was a lot more than I expected – and it added up to an extra year of school just to be eligible to take the professional exam.

> **QUESTION:**
>
> What are the requirements for the job you want?

If you don't know what the requirements are then how can you possibly do a cost benefit analysis?

What about the credentials that other applicants have who are trying to get the same job you want? Surprisingly, almost everyone, even the adjunct professors teaching at the community colleges in California, have a PhD. I can promise you this: If you spend all the years required to get a PhD so that you can be an adjunct professor at a community college, there is no way you are getting the value out of all that time and money you spent going to school. The job simply does not pay enough to repay your loans. However, many students would believe they only need a bachelor's degree and some experience to get that adjunct job. A PhD is not a requirement of the adjunct professor job, but since so many people with them are applying, you will likely not make the list for an interview if you don't have one.

If you have a job in mind, know what the degree requirements are for that job. Is a master's degree required, or more credit hours like the CPA exam? Are others in the field applying with more advanced degrees? You need to research your field of interest to determine *"the what"* that is necessary for you to obtain the job you seek.

The 'What' College Value Analysis

Question 3:

If you know what job you want after you graduate, what is it and what degree or degrees will you need to obtain it? If you don't know, what job do you know that someone else has that you would like to do?

____

____

____

____

What does the job pay – starting salary through 10 years of experience?

Year 1 ______________

Year 5 ______________

Year 10 ______________

Question 4:

How much of the additional value of what you will earn are you willing to give up getting your degree? (Mary is giving up about 40% of all her additional earnings.) Assuming the additional value is $550k of earning, how much of **Your Future Earnings** are you willing to give up getting that degree?

___________%

One additional item that may change your perspective on how much of your future earnings you are willing to give up for your degree is taxes. Taxes always come first. If you consider that you will likely pay 25 – 40% of your income in taxes, you may decide that giving up a high percentage of your income to student loans is not very appealing. Taxes never seem real until you look at your paystub and then they are immediately frustrating. It's the same with student loans, they don't matter when you sign up, they matter a lot when the first bill comes and you realize those bills will come for years if not decades.

The 'What' of College Value Explored

Knowing what you want to do is not extremely important. Most of the interesting people I know still don't know what they want to do with their lives. But as a thought exercise, it is good to put the facts in front of you for what you can expect in additional earnings versus what you are going to spend for that opportunity. Once you pay the tuition, you can't get that money back, and a degree is no guarantee that you will get the additional earnings.

This unfortunate fact is especially true for students who want to help others. A great example is students who want to become teachers. A teacher's salary is typically on the lower end when it comes to earnings. The lifestyle may be attractive, especially if you are also raising children, but it doesn't make any sense to pay full tuition to the best university in the world when the job pays $40,000 to $50,000 per year. The cost doesn't justify the end benefit. You don't buy a Ferrari to commute to work unless you have endless amounts of disposable income, because it's not worth giving up vast amounts of your future earnings when a reasonably priced car gets the job done.

We need to have some salary estimates for our desired career, and we need to be realistic about how long it will take to get there. We have to be willing to work at the *job we can get*, so we can eventually move up to the *job we want.* It is wiser to go to a smaller, state college if you're going to be a teacher than the top-ranked, expensive liberal arts school. While we may not like it, the right answer is not to burden your future with a huge student loan payment.

The other idea to explore here is that if you don't know what you want to do for a career, then you should be very cautious about spending large amounts of money on your education. Not knowing what you want to do is just fine, but perhaps a community college may be a better place to explore different classes to see what interests you, rather than spending $30,000 a year or more at a liberal arts school while you figure it out.

When I ask most of my friends and colleagues what they did their first two years of college, the answer is, almost for everyone, "party, a lot!" I'm all for having fun, and I did my share of partying, but it didn't cost me $30,000 per year. You can get a job, go to school, and party at the same time and still have no debt.

Additionally, we need to discuss the amounts of bricks in our backpack (debt) that can be carried based on profession. We can't pretend this doesn't matter; it certainly does. If you are going to be a doctor, you're likely to make a lot of money once you get done with school, but you'll also need to make a lot of money because you'll have a ton of bricks to carry. But with that higher salary, more bricks are more manageable. The same goes for engineering. A good engineering school can land you a better paying job right out of college, which might mean it makes sense to take out some debt to get there, especially if you get on the job sooner. But if the job you will get out of school doesn't justify the debt, then you're going to be paying off that debt for a very long time, and it becomes more likely you end up like—you guessed it—our good friend, Mary.

By exploring your future salary and income, you can begin to assess the value of what you are buying from the university. We wouldn't have a student loan debt crisis if everyone was getting a *priceless* education because those loans would easily be paid back. I think what most students who say *priceless* mean, is that they are grateful for the experience they had. Assuming you wouldn't trade it for anything is disingenuous because, who knows? You might have a much better experience elsewhere. You just don't know what you don't know. Athletes leaving school early like Zion, as well successful people like Steve Jobs and Michael Dell show that *priceless* is not the right word to describe a degree.

> **QUESTIONS:**
>
> Why do we pay the people who *think* they know what we need to learn?
>
> and then not pay, and demand we get paid by, the people who actually do know what skills we need?

Here is an interesting thought exercise: As a student, you will pay large sums in tuition for people to teach you. When you graduate, you get a job, and despite feeling like you just spent four years learning and now you have knowledge. You start the new job, and you realize you don't really know anything, just like I did. The employer must train you before you can really be of use. Last month while in school, you were paying thousands of dollars for someone to teach you things you thought were of great importance. But this month someone is now training you on what is actually essential for you to be a valuable employee, and now you are being paid by them. Why don't we pay employers for the training they know we need for the position? And why are we so willing to pay schools for what they *think* they know when employers are going to have to train us later?

This scenario was 100% true for me right out of college. “What are workpapers?” makes me laugh to this day. I didn't really even know where to start but was lucky enough to have some co-workers who were willing to help me and show me what was needed so the partner could audit my work. The training all made sense, but if required knowledge I didn’t have. It was the first wakeup call that said to me, "Great, you have a degree, and you even passed the CPA exam, but you don't know much of anything!” Almost everyone I know has had the same experience; the real training begins after school is out. But universities like to keep that a secret. It dampens the mood at graduation if you let that little nugget of information out.

Imagine that speech by the luminary at graduation, with everyone in their gowns and parents proudly in attendance:

> "Congratulations on finishing your degrees. Unfortunately, I have bad news for all of you—you don't know anything worth someone paying for it! But the good news is, you can move into the real world and learn something useful. The truth hurts; sorry to give it to you. Good luck!"

Not exactly how you get invited back to speak again, though the message might be quite accurate.

Takeaways on the 'What' of College

- Not knowing what you want to do for a job or education pursuit is just fine, but don't spend a lot of money figuring out what might interest you. Libraries are full of books – find your curiosity and then pursue it.
- Understand what your degree might get you in terms of additional earnings and how much of those earnings you are willing to give up.
- Parents, don't force your kids into college if they aren't ready. The college experience for growing up is not the same as it used to be; it's way too expensive a proposition just to go and figure it out. Don't be blinded by your experience. It's a different world today, and the value proposition has changed, and the consequences of debt are much greater.

PART 3

Let's Learn About YOU!

Learning about ourselves is fun. We get to explore what makes each of us unique and different, and we get to learn about others and how they may see the world differently. It also allows us to look at things we are interested in, which can lead us to answers to some of the questions about career and education.

Two widely used personality profile systems can help you learn about yourself and others. **The first is the Myers Briggs Type Indicator (MBTI), and the second is the Enneagram.** I recommend you take both tests and read all the information available on all the personality types in both systems. It might help you get along better with your family or friends or give you some explanations on why it is challenging to communicate with certain people.

Every time I have done these personality exercises in work settings, they have had positive results. I've gotten a better understanding of my coworkers' strengths and weaknesses, communication style, and even deeper values. When we share results, there's usually a lot of "Oh, yeah! I definitely see that in you!"

You'll learn a lot about yourself and your preferences. When doing these personality quizzes, think of your preferences to be as simple as right-handed versus left-handed. There are no correct answers, and we all can embody many different traits depending on circumstance, but MBTI shows your general preferences. There are some ethics we need to make clear before you jump into MBTI, as this is not a right versus wrong test.

a. Type is not a trait. It will **not** show you a strength of ability or aptitude, just whether or not you have a strong preference.
b. You are your own best judge of your type. If you don't agree with the results, it is considered a bad test, and you should retake it to find your best fit. Many people sit on the cusp, not having a preference between the two traits in question or being equally balanced on a type (for example, balanced extravert and introvert qualities).
c. There is no right or wrong – there is no preference for any trait. No trait prevents you from achieving your dreams, and no characteristic makes you a better person any more than preferring carrots to broccoli.
d. This test should only be done voluntarily. The results are yours, and you should choose to share them if you want to.
e. All types are equally valuable; they just indicate preferences, and there are highly competent individuals in each preference.
f. Results should never be used to screen for employment or promotions, no one type is better than the others at any specific job and personality tests should never be used to assess viability for employment. This is discrimination and will lead to a lack of diversity in organizations.

If you are under 25, this test can change as your personality continues to develop into adulthood. Unless someone has a traumatic life event, they usually stay pretty close to their Type for life. For simplicity, and because there is a lot of information about these tests available online, this will just cover the basics of MBTI.

MBTI is an introspective set of questions that help analyze your psychological preferences and creates a personality profile based on four different dimensions of how you perceive the world around you and make decisions. The general idea is that we all embody all of these traits, but our personality consists of these traits in different measures. Another way to view it is that this shows what your preference is within each set. While it seems like psychology, it is really more of a description of how you see the world broken down into four main themes. Only you can validate the results as fitting, and if you take the test in a different mindset (your role as a student versus as a daughter, for example) then you can get slightly different answers. While no system is perfect, my experience has been that almost everyone, especially when given feedback from their family and peers, confirms their MBTI results.

Here are the themes and general definitions of MBTI:

Extroverted or Introverted (E/I): This preference is defined much as you would think, but with a twist, as it's more about what energizes you. Some people are energized in crowds and big groups, and some people prefer more intimate, small group engagements and become energized spending time alone.

Extrovert Preference (E)	Introvert Preference (I)
Initiating: Action oriented, willing to act as the social facilitator making introductions. Likes to plan and direct social gatherings.	*Receiving:* Thought oriented, prefers to be introduced as social gatherings, dislikes small talk, preferring in depth discussions with an intimate group or one or two people.
Expressive: Easily makes their interests known and share their thoughts and feelings. Seen as easy to get to know.	*Contained:* Prefers to share thoughts and feelings with a small and select few. Harder to get to know because reactions are mostly internal.
Gregarious: Enjoys being around others and groups, has lots of friends and acquaintances and doesn't differentiate between them.	*Intimate:* Limited circle of close, trusted friends. Enjoys one-on-one conversations. Sharp distinction between friends and acquaintances.
Active: Prefers active environments where they can learn by doing, listening and speaking rather than reading and writing.	*Reflective:* Prefers visual, intellectual and mental engagement; learns best by reading and writing.
Enthusiastic: Prefers a lively, dynamic environment, likes being center of attention and sharing stories; has contagious enthusiasm.	*Quiet:* Prefers to be reserved and quiet but has well thought internal responses to what is happening. Sometimes has difficulty expressing inner experience so may not speak about it.

Sensing or Intuitive (S/I): This preference is about how you gather information and how you interpret information. Those who prefer sensing focus on what can be perceived by the five senses and trust those senses. Those who prefer intuition focus on patterns and interrelationships.

Sensing (S)	Intuition (N)
Concrete: Focuses on tangible, literal perceptions, communication, learning and values. Trusts what the senses tell them and is cautious about things not supported by facts.	*Abstract:* Focuses on concepts and ideas and includes abstract meanings. Prefers symbols and metaphors to facts to explain their views.
Realistic: Prefers things that have tangible benefits. Value efficiency, comfort and security.	*Imaginative:* Values possibilities over tangibles and likes ingenuity for its own sake. Resourceful and good problem solver.
Practical: Likes working with known materials and applying practical, known methods. Prefers modest returns over risky opportunities.	*Conceptual:* Likes knowledge for its own sake and focuses on concepts more than applications. Enjoys complexity and implied meanings and likely to take bigger risks for larger gains.
Experiential: Trust lived experiences as truth and learns best from direct experience. Focuses more on past and present than future.	*Theoretical:* Sees relevance beyond the tangible and trusts theory as having a reality of its own. More future oriented, seeing patterns and interconnectivity among abstract concepts.
Traditional: Prefers continuity, security and social affirmation provided by traditions, institutions and familiarity.	*Original:* Values unique and clever ideas put into use and enjoys demonstrating their originality. Believes sameness has less meaning.

Thinking and Feeling (T/F): this preference is about how you make decisions.

Thinking (T)	Feeling (F)
Logical: Believes that logic and hard data make for the best decisions with a focus on cause and effect, pros and cons.	*Empathetic:* Believes that a decision's impact on people is most important, focuses on values and relationships and trusts their own appraisal.
Reasonable: Uses logic, fairness and impartiality in decision making and clearly defines objectives and decisions.	*Compassionate:* Considers the different needs of all individuals rather than objective criteria and uses their own values as a basis for decisions.
Questioning: Asks questions to understand, clarify and gain consensus to solve problems and find flaws in all viewpoints.	*Accommodating:* Values harmony and using all viewpoints as a more effective way to gain consensus than questioning, challenging and confrontation.
Critical: Uses impersonal critiques of ideas, situations and questions to arrive at truth and avoids flawed ideas and plans.	*Accepting:* Uses kindness and tolerance to arrive at mutually agreeable plans; open to a wide range of ideas and beliefs.
Tough: Stands firm on decisions that have been thoroughly considered and analyzed and wants them to be implemented quickly and efficiently.	*Tender:* Uses gentle persuasion to gain others' agreement and implement new plans and ideas.

Judging and Perception (J/P): This preference is about how you prefer to relate to the outside world.

Judging (J)	Perceiving (P)
Systematic: Prefers orderly and systematic methods at home, work and in play. Values preparation and dislike surprises. Enjoys closure that comes with making a decision.	*Casual:* Likes taking things as they come and prefers to leave options open, delaying decisions as long as possible.
Planner: Likes making long-term plans for the future including social calendar. Feels as though things will not happen as preferred without planning.	*Open-Ended:* Likes flexible plans and freedom to choose in the moment. Doesn't like being committed to long-range plans and prior commitments.
Early Starter: Prefers to plan for a deadline by working steadily to completion, dislikes stress of last minute work.	*Procrastinator:* Works best when pressured by deadlines. Effective at bringing together ideas and enjoys pressure of last minute work.
Scheduled: Likes the comfort and security of working in a routine that is predictable.	*Spontaneous:* Works best with a constant variety of tasks and freedom to decide what to do and when. Feels constrained by routines.
Methodical: Organizes and details plans with listing of sequential items and subtasks to complete in order to accomplish goals.	*Emergent:* Starts tasks without a detailed plan, trusting that a solution will happen to bring the plan together regardless of starting point.

Learning About You Questions

Question 5:

What is your personality type? Do you agree with the description of you? What parts do you agree with? Which parts do you feel are inaccurate?

Question 6:

What types of things are you interested in learning?

Question 7:

Based on what you have learned about yourself and your interests, what jobs currently interest you? Which jobs do you think would be a good fit for your personality type?

Question 8:

Do you feel pressure from your family to obtain a college degree? From whom and what does it feel like? (again, I recommend these questions be completed separately by parents and children and then discussed together)

Learning About You, Explored

There are a lot of people floundering in the world who don't know themselves very well and can't seem to figure out why. Learning about yourself can be a tremendous help in deciding what you study, deciding what type of job you might like, and what type of company you might want to work at. If you're an introvert, you might feel exhausted if you are serving tables all day, or out doing sales. And vice versa, if you are an extrovert trapped in a cubicle writing code all day, you could become very frustrated and not understand exactly why you are unhappy with your job. Knowing ourselves helps us make better decisions, and better decisions lead to a happier life and greater well-being.

Personality tests have definitely helped me understand myself, my wife, parents, coworkers, and even siblings and in-laws better. I'm always amazed when I meet college graduates who don't know their personality type and have not spent any time understanding others. It's good to know that we all see the world differently and it is important to understand there is not one way to see the world that is right or wrong and no one group has better outcomes than others.

Knowing ourselves is also a valuable tool when it comes to pushing back on familial pressure, especially when your dreams for your future and their dreams for your future are not aligned. Family pressure can come in many forms. Some parents live vicariously through their children and view their success as a parent based on the accomplishments of their children but seen through their personality traits. Hasan Minhaj has a joke about his father wanting him to be a doctor so bad that his dad liked everything with the word *doctor* in it. When he told his dad he was listening to Dr. Dre, his dad said, "Very good! This will help you become a doctor!" We can't force personality traits any more than we can force height.

For parents, understanding your child's personality type, and your own, can help a lot. Putting pressure on your child to achieve specific accomplishments won't usually help them succeed but it can often lead to them feeling like a failure. Is Hasan a failure because he became a famous comedian instead of a doctor? His dad may think so, but very few of us thrive under family pressure. Many parents wanted their children to grow up and be just like they were, but that's not typically what succeeds, in an evolutionary sense. Evolution likes for things to be different, and these differences make for the survival of the species. Practically speaking, our lives improve when we get to interact with and learn from people who think and behave differently from us.

When we look at the results of our personality tests and discuss the results, we gain a better understanding of ourselves and the people we love. This allows us to be more supportive and realistic in our expectations. It means that parents shouldn't try to choose the career or life path for their child just as they can't choose their interests, talents or abilities. Each of us comes pre-packaged with our own preferences and interests, as well as weaknesses; I like to think the flaws are by design.

Let's be clear: this doesn't, however, mean parents don't get to have a say, especially when it comes to the effort their offspring puts forth. No personality type gets a free pass to be lazy. If you are going to college the most important thing in the outcome of your education will be your effort.

Johnson O'Conner Aptitude Assessment

Another tool students should consider is the Johnson O'Conner Aptitude Assessment. I have not taken this test, but it has many people who attest that it can help with aptitude assessment for potential career choices. Consider as many options as you can to get to know yourself and your interests.

The Academic You

Now that you have learned more about yourself, we get to the more difficult part of knowing thyself in the context of academics.

Since this is a manual about making the right choice for college, we need to address all the parts of you that should go into making this decision. This means we must not only look at the scores that you will be judged on, but also explore why these might not be as important as everyone says.

The Academic You Questions:

Question 9:

What is your GPA? __________

Question 10:

What is your SAT or ACT score? ____________

Question 11:

Where does your score rank you nationally?

__________%

How does your high school rank? _______

Exploring Your Academic Self

While most of the top universities will defend the use of GPAs and test scores as the basis for their admissions, they really are not as relevant as they would have you believe. The first thing to know about grades is that they are usually indicative of effort and not ability. We all know the kids who fight with teachers about every grade, who always do every homework assignment, ask for extra credit assignments, and have perfect attendance. We also know the other kids in the class who might have a greater ability but put forth a lot less effort and therefore have lower grades.

> **MYTH:**
>
> Test scores measure aptitude and ability.
>
> The truth is that test scores measure your ability to succeed on tests. There are many facets to intelligence, and most cannot be measure by testing.
>
> The truth is that effort and grit will determine your success.

A popular saying is that 'A' students end up working for 'C' students. There are many theories on this, but most of it comes down to the idea that the 'A' students are putting forth great effort, and the 'C' students are doing just enough to graduate. Those 'C' students who have found a passion are spending their time building skills that translate into the real world, versus spending their time to get better grades. Many of the largest companies today were founded by dropouts who felt that the academic system was holding them back. This group includes Michael Dell (Dell), Steve Jobs (Apple), Jack Dorsey (Twitter), Larry Page (Google), Jeff Bezos (Amazon), Ted Turner (CNN, Turner Networks), Steven Spielberg and Oprah Winfrey. They wanted the freedom to pursue their own ideas and innovation, and they are the founders of some of the largest companies in the world.

One of the best examples of someone not applying themselves at all early in life and having terrible grades but completely changing that later in life is Hugh Herr. Hugh was a world-class climber in his youth who got terrible grades in high school because he was focused on being a great athlete and lacked interest in school. While climbing he suffered an accident that resulted in a harrowing rescue that took the life of one of the rescue members, and left Herr with frostbite that required both his legs to be amputated.

After his legs were amputated, Herr realized that the prosthetics available were of very poor quality and did not allow him the mobility he needed to start climbing again; so, he began designing his own. Determined to improve prosthetics in order to help change others' lives and to honor the man who died to save his life, Herr began studying in earnest. He now had a *reason*, and that gave him great focus—the kind of focus that would propel him to a master's degree at MIT and a Ph.D. from Harvard. Today, he is a professor at MIT with one of the most advanced prosthetics labs in the world.

Without the accident, it is unlikely Herr would be a professor at MIT. His life is a perfect example to show that high school grades are not indicative of ability. He also didn't get his undergraduate degree from a prestigious university because he didn't have the grades to get in. He didn't let being turned down by more prestigious schools deter his vision for his future. Instead, he went to the local school, where his desire and focus helped him get excellent grades that eventually allowed him to pursue advanced degrees at MIT and Harvard.

Much of the current education system is not centered on critical thinking and problem solving, but on the regurgitation of information. The teacher assigns a book, reinforces its ideas, and students are tested on their ability to recall the information on a test. Many people are bored by what schools offer and a strict curriculum doesn't interest them. Many professors are heavily trained in research but not so much in teaching, so they struggle to make information interesting. When the information is not of interest, many people put forth just enough effort to get through the class. Others focus a lot of energy on getting high grades because the grades are a reward unto themselves as they are often what makes the parents proud. On the opposite side of this are students who choose to get poor grades to rebel against their parents and the current institutions in place.

Standardized test scores are also part of the game that universities play for rankings. Test scores seem only to help the affluent, and they are a contributing factor of this crisis because they are so highly valued in the ranking system.

Rankings are important to schools because parents and students continue to believe that the **secret formula carried by US News and World Report is important.** So long as that cycle continues, test scores will be a big part of admissions. These scores and the testing system are inherently fallible. The statistics show us that tutors can manipulate these scores, and universities like to use them as a way to admit students with grades that are not as high, but who have parents with bank accounts who can pay the tuition. This will be discussed more later, but the fact that many students who don't belong at elite schools can get in based on their ability to pay for tutors to improve test scores is bad for everyone. It allows students who are not deserving, as evidenced by their poor high school grades and work ethic, into elite schools because their parents can afford a tutor who specializes in test prep. It is a dirty little secret that at many 'prestigious' schools that appear to hold high academic standards are actually full of lazy rich kids whose parents got them a tutor and who can afford to pay tuition. You'll know these students when you have a group project with them, where you end up doing most of the work and they get the same grade. More importantly, it prevents a more deserving student with less financial means from taking that spot.

MYTH:

School Rankings Matter

They only matter to inflate our egos and are actually part of the problem.

To rank higher, schools must spend more on each student. To do so, they must raise tuition. Costs rise for the sake of rankings and students take on more debt for unnecessary spending and higher marketing costs. The cycle never ends.

Standardized tests also don't test social skills, which can be the most important skill in the workplace and life. After all, you might be right, but if no one will listen to you because you have undeveloped social skills, then what good can you create from your ideas? People skills are often at a premium in the workplace, where figuring out how to get things done in groups is more important than having the best answers.

The bottom line is, GPA is a decent indicator of how you will do next year at university, while test scores can easily be manipulated by affluent parents who hire tutors. The standardized tests don't measure any of the things that will make you successful after school, such as creativity, social skills, desire, and grit, but they do allow admissions departments an excuse to let in more students with wealthy parents and poor grades.

So how does this affect you in your decision for college?

First, you need to acknowledge where you fit in on the scale of preparedness for college. The more prestigious universities tout higher standards, and if you are not prepared for the academic rigor, it can be very tough to catch up. You may also belong at that prestigious school and come to realize that many of your fellow students shouldn't be there, and that the academic rigor and prestige the school claims come second to their need to generate tuition. Either can be very frustrating as a student and should lead you to question the value of what you are paying for.

If you need to improve your test scores to play the test score game, the Khan Academy is available. It is a free platform that offers online tutoring in test-taking. It will give you many of the same strategies that high-priced tutors will provide you to help you get a better score on your test.

Another, less common way for schools to determine a prospective student's college worthiness, is to look at their life situation, areas of interest and where they excel outside the classroom. The way the student would sell this to schools is to push the idea that once they find the area of academia that interests them, they will pursue it with passion and will work very hard to achieve excellence. While this may be true, it's a tough sell. It is not as hard to sell yourself in an interview down the road, but it is tough for university admissions to deal with the competing interests of students whose parents can afford tuition.

If you're trying to get into the ~~best~~ highest ranked school you can, the athletic analogy can help bring this point into focus. In high school, you might be the best player on your team, but when you go to college, you will likely be the worst player on the team the day you arrive. That's because the pool of talent just shrunk. Less than 3% of high school basketball players get to play in the NCAA. By that math, you would need to be the best player out of three teams of high school students just to be on a team in college. It's unlikely you will be the best player on your college team the first year out of high school unless you are a rare top recruit.

The same can be true in academics. Almost everyone at MIT has perfect test scores and over a 4.0 GPA (how a GPA higher than 4.0 is possible on a 4.0 scale is a discussion for another time), so even if you are valedictorian of your high school, everyone there is just as prepared, if not more. Are you ready to spend every day in that type of academic rigor? If you are, then good for you, but if you are not prepared for that type of rigor then it is not an environment that you are going to enjoy. If you got a 4.0, but your school is not a great one, then it's also possible your classes will not have prepared you the same as other students attending private or better ranked high schools.

On the other hand, if you think you just got into a prestigious liberal arts school and you expect that everyone else admitted was held to the same rigorous standards, you may also be disappointed. The real admission criteria are who has enough money to pay tuition, and your classes and group work are not worth the value you are paying, as it's likely some of your classmates just don't care but have wealthy parents.

What is essential for you is that you put yourself in a position to thrive in college. To have a great college experience, you need to be engaged, have support and be allowed to mature and learn at your pace. It also helps to believe you are receiving good value for your money.

If you choose a school where everyone is more prepared than you, you will likely not feel supported, and it will be challenging to stay engaged while constantly trying to keep your head above water. You will feel like the kid chosen last for the team. Make no mistake, everyone knows that situation when it happens. You know if you are the worst player and no one really wants you on their team, and it's not a good feeling. I've been that player and it never felt good, and it never created an environment to thrive in.

Mindset and grit are more important than raw talent for success

Understanding what is essential for you to succeed is paramount in making the right decision on where to attend. Too often, students want to go to the highest-ranked school that will accept them. Parents and family can be a big part of this pressure, where the family is proud or embarrassed based on where a student is accepted. This kind of attitude adds a lot of unneeded stress on students' sense of self-worth (so parents, please stop yourselves from doing it). If you go to the highest-ranked school you can but you are not as prepared as the rest of the students and your classes are not engaging to you, it ~~could be~~ will likely be tough to thrive there. Let's remember, college is not the end; it is the beginning of education. You want to put yourself into an environment where you can do well, progress, learn some foundations, get a degree, and hopefully leave not too burdened by debt.

Remember, it's just the beginning of your life's education. You don't stop learning in your 20s, and no university can teach you everything you need to know. Many things you can't learn in a classroom.

One last topic to touch upon here is your mental health.

For most students, you want to go somewhere you will be challenged. When you are challenged, it can be overwhelming, especially if that happens right away as a freshman when you are also in the midst of the transition to college, potentially away from your family. There is a potentially significant downside of the feelings of being overwhelmed, which can lead to thoughts of not being good enough, and the temptation to quit will arise. I have seen it academically, and I saw it a lot athletically, especially for freshman and sophomores. If you don't have parental support, find someone who will support you—you'll need it.

In my second year of community college, we started the year with twenty-six players competing for twelve spots on the basketball team. Two players were expected to redshirt (sit out of competing for a year), and four of us were returning from the prior year. When we returned from Christmas break, we had eight players remaining on the team. Some guys couldn't handle not being the star, some got homesick, and some didn't want to go to school. Everyone who just had the grit to keep showing up every day made the team. This is often the case in life. Those with the grit to continue to show up every day get where they want to go, everyone else has an excuse why they left.

Your ***mindset*** will matter a lot to your success in school (and if you haven't read the book of the same name, I highly recommend it). Unless you allow yourself an easy path, you will be challenged, and there will be things that do not come easily to you. From an employer's perspective, this is the part that makes a degree worthwhile. It shows who has the right mindset, who has the grit to continue when they feel despair creeping in. You can do it; you just need to believe in yourself and keep showing up, especially on days when you don't feel like it.

As part of your mental health, make sure you read the section on What are They Teaching. More and more students are returning from university feeling terrible about themselves and the world. Instead of a focus on the great things we have done for humanity since the industrial revolution, the focus on many campuses is determined by the office of Equity, Diversity and Inclusion. While those words sound good, the effect is the opposite.

Make sure you find an environment that is uplifting and believes in equality of opportunity. Find classrooms that encourage debate and stay far away from anywhere where the science is settled and so is the narrative. Unfortunately, too many schools have been captured and are no longer teaching students to become independent thinkers.

Don't be afraid of being challenged, that is how you get the most out of yourself. But, also be honest about the rigor that you are prepared for, finding this balance is the key to finding an institution you can thrive at.

Takeaways on Learning about You

- It can be fun and educational to learn more about yourself and others, and it can help you gain awareness of how others see the world and help you better understand your friends and family.
- Knowing more about yourself and the way you see the world can help you make better decisions about what to study, where to study, and what type of job you may be interested in after school.
- Having honest conversations with your family about your interests can help you be more supported as a student and more supportive as a parent.
- Test scores and GPA should not define your dreams and are not intelligence tests. Experienced tutors can manipulate test scores, and they fail to measure many of the skills needed to be successful.
- If you need to improve your test scores, try Khan Academy.
- You want to be at an institution where you are in at least the top 50% for GPA, so you have an opportunity to thrive.
- Don't believe that just because students got into that prestigious liberal arts school that they are well prepared and actually care about school; it could be they got help with tests, and Mom and Dad have deep pockets.
- Be open to being challenged. Also, be honest about the potential to be overwhelmed.

PART 4
The System of Higher Education

Questions on Your Higher Education Costs:

Question 12:

Have you visited any campuses you have interest in attending? Y/N

____

____

____

____

____

Question 13:

What did they advise you to do? Did any of them ask you about your family's ability to afford the costs or encourage you to seek a lower cost option?

____

____

____

Question 14:

Have you discussed the costs of attendance with any university? If so, what are the costs?

____

____

____

____

____

Costs per Year:

Tuition: $______________

Room and Board: $______________

Activities and Party Budget $______________

Car, Gas & Insurance: $______________

Total Costs per Year: $______________

X 4

Total Costs for Four Years: $______________

Question 15:

Have you ever received or seen any marketing materials from the institutions you visited?

(Commercials, billboards, etc.) If so, what kinds?

____

____

____

The System of Higher Education, Explored

We like to think of the system of higher education as one that exists to help society by educating students and conducting research. Many of the state universities were founded based on land grants from the states, and most states offer some financial support for the schools. Because many of us attended these universities or grew up going to their football and basketball games, we feel connected to the schools. It's the reason college football is more popular than the NFL, and it is why large universities use their sports teams to market their schools. The large state schools usually have extensive alumni networks, and most people who previously attended universities view them in a positive light because they connect them to their youth and the coming-of-age experience.

But if the universities' primary objective is to help society, how do we reconcile that with the current student loan crisis that they have been instrumental in creating? It's tough to do. The cost of attending a university has increased up 550% in the past 20 years, while wages increased by just 135%. Why did it get so much more expensive so quickly?

There are several reasons, but the main reason is that while the government protected all the student loans from being discharged in bankruptcy, it also increased the amounts that students and parents could borrow. This allowed universities to continue to raise tuition without hiring any additional tenured faculty. In fact, the tenured positions have continued to fall, meaning the quality and the educational flexibility of the people who are responsible for the teaching has continued to fall.

Today's universities look much more like corporations than the educational institutions that exist for the benefit of all citizens. Complete with marketing and lobbying departments (often funded through third parties, such as donors), the emphasis on education and scientific research has been replaced by expensive athletic departments, sales teams, and groups of administrators worrying about many things not related to learning.

MYTH:

Schools care about you and want to help you.

They really only care about enrollment, and you are one of many paying customers.

If schools really cared about student outcomes, tuition would not have increased by 550% in the last 20 years, burdening students with a student loan crisis.

...And I would be writing a more interesting book!

Also, lobbying on behalf of universities are the large financial institutions that also benefit from all the increase in student loans. More loans equal more business, and these loans are some of the best performing financial instruments in the marketplace because they are guaranteed. For the banks supplying and administering these loans, business is booming!

The lobbying is important too. Currently, through the American Council on Education, the schools lobby to prevent legislation passing that would change how student loans are handled in bankruptcy. They know that if the government changes the rules, they will have to change their fees, and schools do not want that, even though this is hurting the students (hence the phrase, "student loan CRISIS").

They also lobby to keep "accreditation" from changing to actually have merit. Accreditation is the process whereby schools are reviewed to ensure they meet specific standards, required for them to have access to federal student loans. Currently, schools pay for the accreditation process directly, so it lacks independence by definition. In an article I read recently, the journalist asked an accreditor why a school with a 10% graduation rate could continue, and the reply was, "It is a good thing for the 10% who get degrees." This tells me that the accreditation process is not independent and shows nothing except the universities paid for this boost in status.

Why do universities have lobbying in congress, but students don't? Who is looking out for the students? Ironically, it is student tuition providing the funding for universities to lobby against the students' best interest.

You don't need to look much further than the highest-paid public employee for each state to figure out that the university system has lost its priorities. A simple question: Who are the highest-paid public employees in almost every state? The answer: the football coaches. In Alabama, the team is led by Nick Saban, who makes over $11 million per year! And it is not just the top coach, the ten assistant coaches at Alabama make a combined $6M, averaging more than the university president. So, what is most important at the University of Alabama: football, or your education?

If the football coaches make $17,000,000, and the average professor makes $108,000, the reality of whose bank accounts are growing speaks for itself.

I don't want to dig too far into the details of athletics, the mistreatment of athletes, and the highly corrupt monopoly of the NCAA, but let's just consider it to be a business. The student athletes get paid the cost of room and board ($26,000/year), then the 85 players on the Alabama football team earned a total of $2.21M, while the coaches made $17M.

In contrast, the Denver Broncos payroll for players is $209M for 53 players, and the highest-paid NFL coach makes $8M per year. So how do we justify paying the players next to nothing while the universities and coaches make millions? I don't think a realistic answer exists for this extortion. The players are not getting their fair share, and the universities should be focused on science and teaching, not winning football games that are used as marketing material. It is easy to conclude that this system is not about the players or academics, and when coaches are paid more than professors and

MARKETING:

Schools have lobbying and marketing departments to sell students, supported by rankings and indoctrination that all students need to go to college.

Who is looking out for the students as costs rise and debts soar?

researchers, what does that say about the priorities of the universities? Roll Tide Roll! as they like to say in Tuscaloosa.

It's important to understand that the university system has become closer to that of a for-profit company than an educational institution, but we've been sold on the idea that a university is where you are exposed to great ideas, have debates, seek truth, and become a better person. In reality, that's less and less of what students are getting.

Don't take my word for it; read the research yourself.

A Gallup-Purdue study looked at the links from college to work and your personal well-being. While we are told that where we go to school is very important and we should celebrate over gaining admission to top-ranking schools, the truth is very different.

Just look at the percentages of students who *agree* with these statements:

1. I had at least one professor who made me excited about learning. (64%)
2. My professor cared about me as a person (27%)
3. I had a mentor who encouraged me to pursue my goals and dreams. (22%)
4. Those who *strongly agree* with all three statements above: 14%
5. I worked on a project that took a semester or more to complete (32%)
6. I had an internship or job that allowed me to apply what I was learning in the classroom. (29%)
7. I was extremely active in extracurricular activities and organizations while attending college. (20%)

Those who *agree* with all three experiential statements (4-6): 6%

Those who agree with all six statements: 3%

A **mere 3%** of people say that college is everything it was supposed to be! How can that be correct, if everyone keeps going? We have a satisfaction rate of 3% to compare against the 94% of parents who believe their child will graduate from college. This is a massive disconnect between what society thinks and what is actually happening.

If we look at Question 13 from earlier in the chapter on advice to families for any institutions you might have visited, how many of them told you it was best to look at all your options and make the best choice based on you and your family's finances? If any of them said yes, then you got lucky and spoke to a decent human being. What is the usual message? "This is the perfect place for you to pursue your dreams!"

Don't worry about the cost; our "aid" package will help you through. The debt you pick up along the way is typically not mentioned. After all, salespeople like to stick to the closing points, and discussing future burdens on students and their families is not the image they want you to have during your visit.

MYTH:

Where you go to college matters.

The truth is that *what* you do when you get to campus is more important than *where* you attend.

CEOs don't care where you went to school, they care about what skills you have.

Regardless of what you are interested in studying and regardless of your family finances, every university is making the same sales pitch, and you need to know that it is just that—a sales pitch, and a highly refined sales pitch at that! They are trying to sell you on their campus, their rankings, and the potential for you to achieve what previous graduates have. "Just look at all the successful people who have studied here," and, "don't you want to follow in their footsteps?" Large companies often roll out the red carpet for interns, showing them a great summer of events and baseball games. All that ends when the real job begins. But just like when you arrive at the office to start a real job, when you arrive on campus, you are now a number, helping the university admissions counselor fill their quota. Once they have your money, they move on to fill the next year's quota.

This may not apply to Ivy League schools and other select top tier universities, commonly referred to as Ivy Plus, but outside of those, *where you go to college is not as important as what you do there*. Both the Gallup-Purdue research and many other articles detail how the college experience is what you make of it and where you went to school matters much less than the type of person you become. This is important to recognize. ***Just as the car you drive does not dictate the person that you are, the school you graduate from does not indicate your potential.***

But a car salesperson would like you to believe differently—if you buy the more premium model, it is because you're a more "premium" person. University salespeople will sell you the same story, just based on rankings and how they are the perfect place for you to achieve your goals. It is also likely that your peer students and their parents will also sell you on the ranking proposition because they too believe that narrative. Now is a good time to reiterate that a degree is not the goal. It is often a part of the goal, but the goal is not to just go to school, the goal is to get a foundational education and then get a job. The job and your career path opportunities are the goal. Learning to ask questions and learn like Socrates is the goal.

In April of 2019, the Chicago Tribune put out a telling article where they asked ten different CEOs of Chicago-based companies how important it was where an employee went to school. **Not a single CEO was interested in where their employees went to school.** All of them care if you, as a person, can work well in a team, care about the work, are passionate, have a good work ethic, and well-developed people skills. Last I checked, they can't teach you how to care, have passion, how to have a work ethic, or work well with others if that's not in your personality. If you are going into an interview, these are the skills you should emphasize.

This is so important to the entire experience that I want to emphasize it as loudly as possible: **UNIVERSITY CANNOT TEACH YOU SKILLS THAT YOUR FUTURE EMPLOYER WANTS YOU TO HAVE!**

The reality is that a university cannot teach you most of the skills you need to develop, so that's why it often doesn't matter which school you attend. What is more important is that you are engaged and interested, so you put forth effort—hopefully inspired effort like Hugh Herr. As an example, consider the following thought exercise: How do you know when to fire someone who is not fitting into your organization? How can you teach this skill?

As a small business owner who has hired and fired many people, this is not a straightforward answer. Asked to 100 people, I would expect at least 75 different answers. The honest answer is that you cannot teach this skill, it can only be learned experientially. Skills are developed over time based on your experience and your intuition in a particular job situation.

Sometimes people require more training or need to know what actions are not appreciated by their colleagues. Often flaws in the hiring process need to be refined as people are fired or let go because they do not fit. Everyone does not fit into every organization. If you are building a team and Shaquille O'Neill is your center, you don't need another star center, but HR might have just hired you one anyway. If you cannot utilize the new person's skills, then better to let them go on to another organization that can. Being fired may be the best thing that happens to a person even though it may not feel like that in the moment.

The point here is to engage in a topic that cannot be taught in a classroom. How to build your team and when to let people go is a skill that cannot be taught. Case studies might help, but until you are living in that situation, with staff coming in your office to complain about the new person not working out and you are trying to figure out why they are not fitting in, you can't teach someone this skill, it is something you have to learn through experience.

But none of the universities like to talk about these skills because their programs don't address them, and they are hard to teach and harder to evaluate whether or not you possess them. They hope that you pick up many of these life skills as part of your maturity, but they have no way to measure them. Just like sales itself, there is no class on passion or work ethic. There is no test to show if you get along well with others or if you care. We would like to believe that the interview process will help us figure out who to hire and who will fit in, but there is no guide on how to develop the skill of when to let people go.

In my research, where you attend college matters only in a few specific situations. The Ivy League and the Top 10 schools are exempt. Not because you will learn specialized knowledge—

they don't have secret books that the rest of us don't have access to as exposed in *Good Will Hunting*—but because of the amount of resources spent on each student, who you will meet while you are there, and the high standards to get in are different. For some people, the alumni network matters. There are many schools with extensive alumni networks, and if you went through the same programs they did, it might help you get an interview. The other exceptions are typically for graduate degrees. Where you went to law school can matter for the type of law you want to pursue, and medical schools also have similar specialties.

For the majority of jobs, where you went to school will continue to matter less and less as you age, just as the Chicago CEOs described. At some point it becomes irrelevant because, like my friend getting her MBA, you will have learned so much after college that what you learned in school becomes insignificant, and it will not even be included in the interview process. Five years out of school, the question is, "What can you do?" not "Where did you go to school?"

Employers are also beginning to rethink degree requirements for many jobs. A recent WSJ article detailed how Alphabet, Delta Airlines and IBM have reduced educational requirements for certain positions and are shifting hiring to focus more on skills and experience. *The persistently tight labor market has accelerated the trend that builds on a debate about the benefits and drawbacks of encouraging more people to attend four-year colleges and as organizations try to address racial disparities in the workplace.* What they are really saying is the same thing that the CEO's in the Chicago are saying: skills and ability matters, not the piece of paper.

Referring back, Question 13 asks you if anyone you met on campus asked you about your ability to pay and your family finances. I would even take that one step further: **Did anyone ask**

you if you had a goal to limit the amount of debt you were willing to incur to go to college?

It's vital for you to understand that these institutions only care about you while they are selling you on their campus and the best quad for you to enjoy while you pursue your dreams. Just like at a car dealership, if you are only interested in test driving and you're not going to buy, they will stop paying attention to you very quickly. ***But if the universities you visit are interested in your wellbeing as a person and as a student after graduation, wouldn't they be discussing all the different ways to keep your***

EVERYONE GETS TOLD:

"This is the perfect campus for you to pursue your dreams."

NO ONE GETS TOLD:

"You could get the same education for way less money at a community college or smaller school."

loans to a minimum? If the credits count the same, wouldn't they discuss that the community college has a pathway to the university as the best value for your family? They should, but they rarely do.

I have a friend who has two boys, both currently attending the University of Colorado studying engineering. My friend does pretty well, and while having both of them in school at the same time is stretching the family finances, he saved a lot for them and, like most parents, would give up everything he had for them to pursue their dreams. When he visited the University of Colorado with his oldest son, he asked if his son would be able to get into the engineering program if he started at a community college. The salesperson (and I am fully aware they refer to themselves as “counselors” but, let's call them what they really are) told them that it would be less likely that his son would be accepted into the engineering school unless he enrolled at the university as a freshman.

Since most of us want to believe that our state universities are looking out for us and these are "our" institutions, my friend believed her. After all, she is the expert who works at the school, so wouldn't she know more than we do? Well, she may know more about how the engineering school works, but what is for sure is she was not looking out for the best financial interest of the family because there is a direct, let me repeat that, a direct line for students to transfer from a community college!

From the University of Colorado School of Engineering webpage:

Students who begin at Arapahoe Community College can transfer directly to CU Boulder to finish their degree in engineering. Thanks to an integrated partnership, this pathway can be attractive to both community college students, as well as qualified high school students taking concurrent enrollment classes with ACC.

CU Boulder Engineering and Arapahoe Community College have designed this pathway to support a more streamlined transition between colleges and give you a detailed view of what your academic plan will look like.

At ACC, you can complete classes before transferring to CU Boulder and have the peace of mind that your credits will apply directly to your engineering degree.

WE PLACE A HUGE VALUE ON GETTING A DEGREE, BUT WE NEVER STOP TO ASK: "WHAT DID THEY *NOT* TEACH ME?"

That difference of information could be huge, especially for a student taking out loans to cover tuition costs. If you can transfer directly and get the same degree, the difference of two years of living at home and paying community college tuition could be *as much **$50,000 in savings***. And you still get the same degree from the same institution. But telling you that information will not help the salespeople fill their quota, so they tell you the story that helps them. A car salesman is not going to tell you that you can get a better deal at a different dealership; he wants to sell you what is in his inventory so he gets paid. The system is not looking out for you, and many schools will make you feel as though you are lucky to be admitted, and you should be happy to pay, regardless of the amount.

Paying out of state tuition usually gets you an even tougher sales pitch from the university. If you are going to pay out of state tuition, typically tens of thousands of dollars more, then you are what is called a "whale." That's a finance and poker term for the person they get to extract a lot of money from. The advice is that it is very, very hard to get your status changed to in-state, so you are likely better off just attending for a full four years here, paying out-of-state tuition every year. This advice does not help the family the most nor does it have the best interest of the student in mind.

What the student loan crisis shows us is that the universities don't really care about the cost to the student and families. They are not concerned with the amount of debt that students sign up for, and they don’t track whether the degree the student earns will ever provide the additional income to justify the loans. They just want your tuition money so they can keep doing what they have been doing, no changes required. Hiring more administrators and increasing costs without increasing the quality or value of the service they are providing. In any other industry, they would be like Blockbuster Video, gone because someone else figured out a better way. Instead, they are protected by government decree.

In some industries, like programming, there are better alternatives already, and it is only a matter of time before universities are shut down, just like Blockbuster. (Kids, if you don't know what Blockbuster was, Google it for a lesson in change. You can also learn about VHS, Betamax, and other obsolete technologies.) All of this gets wrapped up nicely by the universities in how they present themselves to you. They will tell you that you can afford all the costs and they have the perfect "aid" package for you.

How would you define the word "aid"? Write it below.

____

____

____

____

____

____

I'm guessing that missing from your definition of the word *aid* is a promise to repay, with interest, all sums and fees for the loans, including charging loan origination fees and processing costs, compounding interest that begins with your first loan until you begin repayments? Your definition likely does not include these fancy legal words, which equate to a future right to your earnings. Also remember its ***Special Debt*** that you cannot get rid of unless you die or pay it off.

Imagine if the universities had to present their proposal to you this way:

» Tuition: $16,000;
» Room and Board: $14,000.
» Scholarships and need-based aid: $5,000

...and 25% of all your future earnings for the rest of your life.

How many of us are signing up for that package? No way! It doesn't look like *aid* because it isn't *aid*, but that's how they sell it to us. Your debts are now *aid?* Aid is, by definition: "help, typically of a practical nature." Debt is not, cannot be, and should never be described as aid.

At best, it should be described as amounts financed for the student to be repaid after college is completed. Calling it aid should be illegal. This is one additional way that you can know that you are being sold and not helped. Not even credit card companies would have the audacity to call debt "aid." It's a hell of a stretch, rationalized on the notion that education will help you in the future to earn more. But what if it doesn't? What if you paid so much for your education that you can't possibly earn your way out of the debt? What if you don't graduate but still have a lot of loans? Well, first, you are not alone, but you have no recourse. There is no loan forgiveness, so that *aid* they just gave you becomes a weight, just like it became for our friend, Mary.

FACT:

Community college credits count the same towards a degree.

FACT:

Community college credit hours ~~usually~~ almost always cost a lot less!

True financial aid would be money that you don't have to repay. When a natural disaster strikes, we don't send *aid* and then three years later send them a bill for it, complete with compounding interest because that doesn't meet the definition of aid! If schools were required to change the terminology from *aid* to *future earnings you agree to give up,* then perhaps fewer students and parents would agree to the "aid" package and I wouldn't need to write this book.

THINGS THEY SHOULD TEACH BUT DO NOT:

- HOW TO BREATHE
- MONEY AND CREDIT (STUDENT LOAN CRISIS IS A RESULT OF THIS LACK OF EDUCATION)
- FOOD, NUTRITION AND YOUR IMMUNE SYSTEM
- MONOPOLIES AND SPECIAL INTEREST GROUPS POLITICAL INFLUENCE
- WHY DEBATE IS IMPORTANT AND FREE SPEECH IS ABOUT PROTECTING THE SPEECH YOU HATE

Takeaways from Exploring the System of Higher Education

- You are being SOLD! Universities are not here to help you. They are a business, and they are selling you a product. The same as a car. If you let them, they will charge as much as you are willing to pay, but that does not mean you are getting value for your money. Everyone who graduates receives a degree, though not everyone pays the same amount in tuition.
- Sales tactics include a value proposition. They offer you some discounts and call them grants, scholarships or merit aid, but it's all for the same purpose—to make you feel as though you are getting a discount in the hopes that you will ignore the fact that that tuition price is still way too high for the value of the degree.
- Every school will sell you on the idea that their campus is the ideal place for you to pursue your dreams, and they will all roll out the red carpet for the sales presentation. But when you show up on campus, with your tuition paid, you are just another number, filling an enrollment slot.
- If coaches are the highest-paid employees on campus, then what's most important, education or sports?
- Tuition keeps rising because everyone keeps paying, and the government continues lending. There is a lot of money going into lobbying and marketing, but that money is not going to hire more tenured professions or to improve your education.

Dirty Secrets that Universities Don't Want You to Know

Unveiling the business of education is so crucial that this section has a second part, because this is the information they don't want you to discuss or inquire about, and they certainly don't want families to ask more questions. They want you to feel that you are *lucky* to be accepted, that it is very competitive, and other students are waiting in line if you don't want your spot. They want your decision to be based on fear and not the value proposition.

Questions on Dirty Secrets Universities Don't Want You to Know

Question 16:

Are you aware that community college credit hours count the same at the university, and they are often required to be accepted at state universities by law?

____

____

____

____

Question 17:

Do you know the average class size at the university you want to attend for freshman and sophomore classes? What are the average class sizes?

____

____

Question 18:

What do you think the average class size is at a community college?

____

____

Question 19:

Can you think of any reasons why a community college class might be better than a university class?

____

____

____

____

Question 20:

Is living on campus the best environment for learning for an 18 or 19-year-old? Y/N

____

____

____

What are the pros and cons of a dorm room versus living at home for each of the following?

- » A quiet place to study
- » People who love you holding you accountable
- » Food – quality and healthiness
- » Friends – spending time with and meeting new friends
- » Problems with roommates
- » Freedom to explore being an adult
- » Add other topics you think are important

Dorm Room Pros

Dorm Room Cons

____
____
____
____
____
____
____
____
____
____
____
____
____
____
____
____

Question 21:

What percentage of college graduates have a job related to their degree 10 years after graduation? __________%

Suckers Pay Retail

Another thought experiment: You and I are each going to purchase a car. Not just any car, but the same car, with the same options, because we are besties, and we want to show the world we like the exact same thing. We are each going to go through the car-buying process on our own, and then we are going to discuss our experiences afterwards and share all the details. The vehicle we'll purchase is a brand new Honda Accord, sport model. We decide we won't talk to each other until we both have the cars in the driveway so we can compare the experiences.

You go to the closest Honda dealership, accept that there is no negotiating, and that they have precisely what you want on the lot. They are willing to work out financing on the spot so you can get everything done that day. The salespeople were very friendly, the test drive went well, your salesperson is interested in many of the same things you are and tells you this car, "is a great value for the price, and you can drive it for decades to come." You don't read much of the fine print since the price and the financing you are told is "similar to competitors", and you leave happy because you got what you wanted, and the experience was quick and easy.

I take a different course of action. I call up every dealer within 100 miles. I tell them exactly what I want and get quotes from all of them. I ask when the next sale will be and when the last sale ended. I ask them about lease specials and financing options. I wait until the car I want has been on a dealers' lot for a long time and then go back to negotiate. I don't like the financing options they quoted, so I go to my credit union and get my own financing. It takes me a bit longer to get the deal done. Meanwhile, you won't stop texting me, asking me when I'm going to finish so we can show everyone our identical cars.

Finally, I complete the purchase, and we both start showing up to events with the same car. It's a great time, and we both have a learning experience and a story and a great car. A few months later, we sit down and do a deep dive into our experiences and the deals we each got. You paid about $1,000 under sticker price at the no-haggle dealership and financed your car at 6% APR through the offer from the dealership. Your cost for the vehicle was $34,000, and with sales tax added and at a 6% interest rate with payments over seven years, the total you will end up paying is $45,848.29.

Your Honda	**My Honda**

MSRP: $35,000	**MSRP: $35,000**
Price Paid: $34,000	**Price Paid: $31,000**
Interest Rate: 6%	**Interest Rate: 3.9%**
Total of All Payments: $45,848	**Total of All Payments: $37,868**
Difference in Payments: $8,000 or 20% Less	

Because of my willingness to wait and haggle, I got the price down to $31,000, and my credit union financed the car at 3.9%. Over the same seven years, with sales tax added, my total payments will be $37,868. That's almost an $8,000 difference, or 20% less, for the exact same car. I wish we had not gone through our deep dive because now you are upset at me because I didn't get you the same deal that I got.

I use this example because it's one we can easily identify with, as there is a tangible product that is the same. None of us wants to pay more for the same car, but when it comes to paying for a 4-year degree, it happens every day. As with my friend and his son at the University of Colorado, they don't want to advertise that you can basically get 50% off your bill for your degree by going to a community college for two years first.

In fact, they will usually tell you the same thing they told my friend, that it is *NOT* as likely you will get into the program you want if you don't spend all four years with them. But this just isn't true. Most states require that community college credits transfer, and most community colleges have direct programs to transfer into specific majors at the state colleges, just like Arapahoe Community College and the University of Colorado. And while some community college courses will not count because they are preparatory courses for the credits that do, most of the credits will transfer. Take my word for it; I did it!

If a community credit course counts the same but costs a fraction, then what are you paying for? Good question. That's why it's a dirty secret. The secret is that the diploma does not come with an asterisk that says, "two years at community college." The degree says the same thing for me, who went to a community college, as it does for the person who went to the university for all four years.

What they don't want you to know is that as a freshman at a major state university, your class sizes will be huge, often in the hundreds. Think about your high school class size. Most state education systems recommend a high school class size of no larger than 30, with an average recommended class size of 23 students. So, when you are 18, it is recommended your class size be less than 30, but at 19 it can be in a lecture hall with hundreds of students? And it costs thousands of dollars more? For comparison, the average class size at a community college is 25-35 students. Which students do you think will get more personalized attention?

Another dirty little secret universities don't like to discuss is the answer to Q19: Can you think of any reasons why a community college class might be better than a university class? A smaller class size definitely seems like a benefit for learning. Here are a few other ideas on why a community college class might be more beneficial to you than a university class. Comparing costs is an easy one, but what about who is teaching the course?

It might be the same teacher at both the university and the community college. As discussed earlier, despite the considerable increase in costs, there are fewer tenured professors on campus, so more classes are taught by adjuncts, especially freshman and sophomore classes. Or your class may be taught by a graduate assistant, usually someone who is pursuing a graduate degree but likely has little real-world experience to share. Wouldn't you rather learn from someone who knows, who has done it? I'd prefer a tax class taught by someone who worked at an accounting firm or for the IRS, versus a graduate student with no experience, working on their master's degree.

Community college courses are often taught by people with a lot of real-world experience who just don't happen to have a Ph.D., but they usually have a lot of practical lessons that are very valuable. I'm not going to use this platform to attack the tenured professors with a Ph.D., but I do want to discuss what a Ph.D. means. A Ph.D. is a degree in research. It means that that person understands how to do research. It does not make them a better teacher, and it does not mean that they have practical experience that will help them teach you many of the things you want to know and need to learn. Remember all of the things that they can't teach you? Many of the adjunct professors I had were great because while they didn't have a Ph.D., they had experience and a passion for teaching. Most Ph.D.'s are interested in doing more research and getting their research published. That does not help you as an undergraduate student.

Another major factor in learning is who is in the classroom. As a freshman at a large university, you are likely to be surrounded by people exactly like you–18- to 19-year-olds with little real-world experience in pursuit of a 4-year degree. Community colleges are full of all sorts of people at different stages of life and not all in pursuit of a four-year degree. Many are there to learn valuable job skills, and many of these people have relevant life experiences from which you can learn.

Now let's look at Question 20: Is living on campus the best environment for learning for an 18- or 19-year-old? Dorms are not great places to learn to grow up. They are filled with young people, with undeveloped brains (that continues until about age 25), often on their own for the first time, and many make bad decisions and are influenced by peer pressure and a surplus of drugs (that includes alcohol as it is a drug). Now, I'm not one to say don't have a good time—college should be fun—but this is a discussion on what would be a better environment for learning. With the hefty price tag of tuition and campus living, if you wish to just have fun, then go take a gap year, get a job and do that first—not while paying high cost tuition.

Living at home has its downsides and may not feel like the best college experience but being around people who love you and who will hold you accountable for getting to class could help a lot. Which place is better for food? That's almost always going to be at home. No one ever misses dorm cafeteria food!

One of the biggest of the dirty secrets at universities is the standard requirement that freshman students live on campus. They rationalize this as a transition period into early adulthood, where your food is prepared for you, you're in a secure environment, and surrounded by your peers, while ignoring the downsides: the higher cost of housing (especially if you could live at home), the lousy food, the noisy dorm environment, and the likelihood of sexual assault. Most sexual assaults happen in dorm rooms, and first-year students are particularly vulnerable. Aided by copious amounts of drugs, it's easy to see why this happens, and it is something universities don't want to discuss and often try to manipulate in their statistics. Were these things considered as part of the wellbeing of the student on your campus visit? Usually, they leave out the sub-optimal parts and focus on all the lifelong friendships you'll develop. You are not prevented from meeting anyone by living at home, but you might have a parent that helps you make better life decisions.

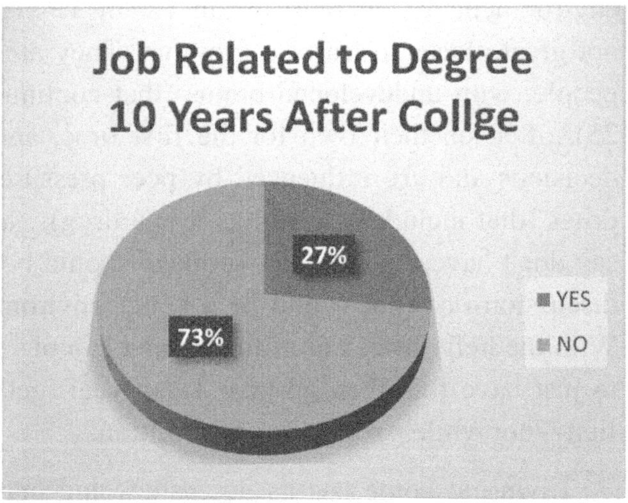

We finish here with Q21: What percentage of college graduates have a job related to their degree ten years after graduation? The question gives us some insight into how important a particular major or degree might be for you.

The research tells us that only 27% of college graduates have a job related to their degree. That includes engineers, doctors, lawyers, teachers and accountants – which doesn't leave a lot of room for much else, so that means most of us will end up with a job that is unrelated to our degree. So, *what* you study does not seem to be nearly as crucial as learning how to learn. We already touched on this, but it is worth mentioning multiple times: Universities cannot teach you all you need to know. There is not a skill called "business" that you magically *know* when you graduate. What you study and what you will learn at a university is just a small amount of what you will need to know to be successful.

DID YOU KNOW:

More aid goes to families with incomes over $100K/year than families under $20K?

How does this apply to students? Don't worry about a minor in this or a double major in that, just get a degree and get out as quickly as possible. I hear student tick off all the minors they need as though they are just life interests and don't have a cost. Your learning should never stop, but that extra semester for a second minor has real costs.

I don't always like being the practical voice in the room, but once you graduate, no one will care what your degree is in or even where you went to school. If you're not likely to have a job that is specific to your degree, the second minor will be genuinely insignificant. My advice is to take extra English and communications classes, as those will help you in whatever field or job you pursue.

One final dirty secret they don't want out there. Most students are offered some sort of "scholarship" or financial aid to reduce their tuition. Sticker price tuition is like the sticker price at a car lot—only suckers pay that price! But how much of a discount does everyone get? Oh, that's something they don't like to talk about and is based on their *proprietary* algorithm. But here is what it comes down to: the "scholarships," "grants," or "aid" that they offer each person are based on what their algorithm tells them they need to provide, so that the family believes they are getting enough value to pay the remaining tuition. This is a pure marketing strategy: Pump up the sticker price and then offer a "sale" or discount. According to a recent New York Times article, American colleges collectively now give more institutional aid to each student with a family income over $100,000, on average, than they do to each student with a family income under $20,000. They have sold us on the idea that this aid is need-based, but the need they are referring to is the school's need to fill that tuition spot, not what is best for families.

This is often part of the "value sale" that universities like to push to parents and students. If they tell you your sticker price is $45,00 per year, but you are getting a scholarship for $25,000 per year, you feel you are getting a great deal. Except that still leaves you with $20,000 per year in tuition plus room and board—not such a great deal. Athletes are especially prone to fall for the value proposition sale when they are pursuing their dreams of a college athletic experience. There is specific information in Supplement #2 at the back of this book on athletic scholarships to discuss this in greater detail.

The Ranking System in Higher Education

A lot of students and parents spend much of their time researching universities, and one of the most used measures for evaluating schools is the *US News and World Report* rankings. We all love ourselves some rankings! We like to rank everything and create awards for no other reason except to promote and claim a higher social status. But here is the downside of rankings: For someone to win, everyone else must lose. I don't want to spend too much time diving into the inner workings of the ranking system as a zero-sum game, as you cannot know the whole of the secret sauce for any ranking systems. But I do want to discuss their role in the current student loan crisis and the increased cost of a degree.

As we have mentioned, universities have increased costs by about 550% in the last 20 years, but they don't spend that extra money on more professors. It's just the opposite, in fact. Overall, the number of tenured professors has declined. This is bad news, as these are the people who have achieved academic freedom of expression that allows them to have their own views and create meaningful discussions for learning. Where is that addressed in the rankings?

The rankings are a game. They will have nothing to do with your education. The primary factor for rankings is the amount of money that schools spend "on" students. Now, if they used specific measures, like the number of classes taught by tenured professors across universities, that might be a useful metric. Instead, schools report how much they spend on each student, so they get to decide which expenses count as being spent "on" students.

Does the new football stadium count as spending "on" students because students can attend games and participate in the games? What about all the new administrators? We don't get to know; it is all part of the secrecy of rankings, and they would prefer we "pay no attention to the man behind the curtain" to borrow an old metaphor from a wizard.

> **RANKINGS ARE A ZERO-SUM GAME:**
>
> There can be only a single "Number 1" school. Everyone else is not as good, but they cannot measure what that means.
>
> This is psychological warfare to make you believe rankings are important.
>
> Where are the rankings for students with the least amount of debt and highest wages, by degree?

To me, ranking schools is about as useful as pre-season rankings for sports. It doesn't mean anything except to those who are betting, or in this case, parents and students who want to believe them. Being the preseason #1 team is meaningless. It only means that the people configuring the rankings have decided it so. It is almost as subjective as which movie will win the Oscar. Just because one film wins the award does not mean it will be your favorite movie of the year. What it may mean is that the higher ranked school is more expensive than it should be because it is spending more money, raising tuition, etc., so it can rank higher. I'd rather rank lower in debt than higher in costs. Last time I checked, diplomas don't come with rankings, and the CEOs in Chicago didn't mention rankings in the skills they were looking for in employees.

The reason the ranking game persists is because people react to it. Parents and students get caught up in prestige and the idea that if they go to a higher-ranked school, the experience will be better for everyone. Mom and Dad can brag to friends and family about the prestigious school Junior is attending, but the truth is there is no correlation between the ranking of school and long-term success and happiness. Because people believe in them, schools' rankings determine how many applications a school will receive, so the ruse continues and students pay the price, literally. Have you heard of the student debt crisis?!

It is a system without an end: spend more to rank higher, charge higher tuition, and keep increasing spending and costs every year to keep that high ranking. It only ends when students determine that all that extra money for rankings and bigger stadiums is a waste of their money, and that is why we have a student loan crisis. Ranking of schools, just like the ranking of sports teams, is fool's gold. You can't win a championship in the pre-season, and you don't get a good education because of a school's ranking. You will only get a great education if you care, are passionate about your studies, and get yourself involved.

Another little-known ranking secret is that they sell your SAT/ACT scores to universities. You might think this is a good thing as the university might "find" you, but that is not the purpose. The universities use your own test scores to market to you, not in the way you think, but in a way that keeps their ranking high: they just want your application if you have a high score *so they can reject you*. The more applications they get, the more they can reject, increasing their school's score by lowering their admissions rate. It is a dirty game, but they don't mind making you fill out an additional application to help them.

RANKINGS ARE NOT USEFUL:

The rankings are not based on criteria they (the school counselors) consider necessary to student outcomes.

The ranking formula misleads consumers and has compromised the journalist integrity of the publication.

Although less than 3% of all graduates have experiences in college related to securing great jobs and having great lives (see Gallup News: *Life in College Matters for Life After College*), rankings persist. This shows that what is essential in education is not measured in the rankings. Rankings should only be about what happens after school. If we want to rank schools, shouldn't we look at the lives of everyone who graduated and how much value they attribute to where they went to school? We should evaluate the outcomes and work backward, not look at how much money schools spend during the process. We can always spend more money. Let's have class on a yacht!

What you do in school is what matters. How much you want to learn matters. The ranking of your school will never matter outside of conversations based on status, and status is a zero-sum game that will never lead to a happy life. And if all that doesn't convince you that you can't trust rankings, then what about those who are responsible for admissions? This would be the National Association for College Admission Counseling (NACAC), which includes those who run the admissions departments at colleges and counselors helping students choose a college. Overwhelmingly, as outlined in their own " Report of the NACAC Ad Hoc Committee on US News and World Report Rankings", their members agree that the rankings offer misleading conclusions about institutional quality. They cite "USNWR's 'arbitrary' assignments of weights to each category and subcategory." That means that the NACAC does not agree with the ranking system because it is not based on criteria they consider necessary to student outcomes, but whatever arbitrary criteria USNWR decides to use.

The conclusion of the committee is staggering, and if I didn't read it from the source, I don't think I would believe it, based on discussions with parents and students and how much they believe in these rankings: *"The Committee believes that the research and discussion about the imprecision of ordinal rankings in the 'Best Colleges' list has reached a point where not proactively acknowledging the limitations of the ranking formula through vigorous consumer education and flexible 'ranking' options risks misleading consumers and has compromised the journalistic integrity of the publication."*

To clarify, the people responsible for admissions are telling you that these rankings are misleading and compromise the journalistic integrity of the magazine! They not only say that they believe the rankings DO NOT matter; they think they are misleading you! If you are a parent who feels that rankings do matter, that's a tough bit of knowledge to have to reconcile. The prestige they have you believing in is just a narrative.

The 'What' is More Important than the 'Where'

To further my point that where you go to school doesn't matter as much as what you do while there, recent studies in the value of education from Anthony Cornevale at Georgetown University show that *choosing the right program of study* can matter more than a prestigious diploma when it comes to good starting salaries. They hope to have their work online and updated, so students can compare graduates' starting salaries and debt payment of specific degree programs at various schools, but the data continue to show that what you study can be more important than where.

This is extremely valuable in determining the cost benefit of higher education. Despite the fact that many elite schools have higher student support, students with degrees in biology from Indian River State College (FL), Cal State Hayward and San Jose State University ranked among the top 10 in the country when it comes to graduate earnings with student-loan debt payments subtracted. That's on par with Dartmouth and Columbia! Read: They are a GOOD VALUE.

Similarly, for civil engineering, San Jose State and Cal Poly San Luis Obispo ranked among the top 10 along with Cornell. Students who completed degrees in STEM subjects at smaller schools earned more than those graduating with humanities and education degrees from higher ranked or more selective colleges. The general conclusions of Dr. Carnevale's work match my own: The labor market dictates wages, and students who earn the most after graduation tend to mix general education with career-specific skills.

One of the major findings of this work was something my sister tells me all the time and the data back up: A lot of associate degrees and vocational certificates are great value for higher salaries when compared to the cost to obtain them. The biggest winner is registered nurses. Graduates from Santa Rosa, Butte, Carrington College-Sacramento and Unitek College earn $80,000 plus salaries after earning an Associate degree.

According to Dr. Carnevale, about 30% of graduates with Associate degrees earn more, at least in the short term, than graduates with bachelor's degrees. Where you live and the employers in your area can matter a lot. In Ohio, students earning certificates in industrial technology and electrical engineering earn higher starting salaries than students with bachelor's degrees in more general fields of study. Sometimes the bachelor's degree catches up in salary, but sometimes it doesn't, especially if there is a lot of debt included in the bachelor's degree.

The Ivy League Proposition

There has been a lot of research on Ivy League schools, whom they admit, and the potential for an Ivy League education to offer a path to economic mobility and into jobs that pay in the top 1% of salaries (classified as over $600,000/year). The Ivy League argument is valid, but it is challenging to find comparable data for other schools, making it difficult to ascertain potential outcomes for any individual who could have gone to an Ivy

League school but chose a different one instead. The Ivy League schools would also like everyone to believe that they want the smartest people to attend, regardless of socioeconomic background, but their admissions tell a different story. The data does, however, indicate that if you are from a lower-income family and can get in, the Ivy Plus schools may offer the most opportunity for changing your families' fortune.

The benefits of an Ivy education are simple to discuss. They spend a lot more money, per student, than other schools, often over $100,000 per student, per year. How is this possible when tuition is only $60,000 per year, you ask? Endowments. This is the reason that I believe going to an Ivy League Plus school may be worth the cost and potentially even debt. When Harvard decided to increase its endowment, it set a goal of $6 billion (yes, that's billion, no misprint there). They ended up raising over $9 billion. And since we are exploring the system of higher education, we will ask, who gave all that money? We will likely never get a direct answer to that question, but there is a reason that so many wealthy families can get their children into the Ivy League schools. It's the old money way: They contribute to the university for decades.

Now the schools will tell you that donations are not part of the admissions process, and that legacy only counts a little, but the statistics tell the truth. Wealthy families have access to private schools that act like funnels to elite institutions. They also have access to private tutors and the best test preparation academies in the country. It is easy for the Ivy League schools to justify whom they admit, as they all have high test scores, and high test scores keep up the school's ranking so they can repeat the process. The history of the SAT shows that it was explicitly designed to keep wealthy families' children attending the Ivy

League schools. In short, the system is doing precisely what it was intended to do.

What if your test scores are in the top 1%? Should you apply for an Ivy League school? Do your research. If you come from a low-income family, they may waive the application cost. Moreover, if you are accepted, and your family income does not reach a certain threshold, they may subsidize the full price of school and room and board. That is an incredible deal if you can get it but know that there is also going to be some difficult times at school.

IVY LEAGUE ADMISSIONS ARE NOT A MERITOCRACY:

Legacy enrollment would not be so high if this were not true.

But legacy parents are playing the long game, donating to (read: bribing) the schools in the most old-fashioned of all admissions policies.

Make sure you are aware of the implications of socioeconomic status on campus: The wealth of the other students may be overwhelming to you. Spring break will feel awful, as your classmates' vacation on private islands and go on amazing trips while you struggle to eat because the cafeteria is closed for the week. But if you can get in, and you feel prepared for and desire the academic rigor, then go for it.

However, after you graduate, it will be challenging to get one of those high-paying jobs at "elite professional service" (EPS) firms. They like people who look like them and share similar background stories. You could get lucky, but don't think the system that continually helps the wealthy ends with Admissions. You probably didn't even want one of those jobs until you arrived on campus, where everyone proclaimed the benefits of working at an EPS firm because of the high pay. Follow your own path.

The EPS path comes with new stresses. Most people with jobs in the top 1% of income work all the time. The research may say that the Ivy League is the fastest path from low to high income, but ask yourself: Do I want to be in the top 1% for income and have to constantly put forth commensurate effort to be there? If that is your goal, then keep on pursuing that Ivy League dream. But if what you want is to be able to have a solid middle-class job and have some work/life balance and contribute to your community, then maybe the Ivy League dream isn't worth the stress and the effort. Only you can make this decision.

The Ivy League Degree Mobility Illusion

The more research I do on the topic of college education, one idea continues to stand out: The education system is set up just like every other institution in the world—for the betterment of the wealthy. After all, who writes the rules? We can pretend that college is different, that admissions departments are a meritocracy, and that companies will hire based on what you do in school, but admissions departments are not meritocracies, and neither are employers.

The data show that the select group of people who are admitted to the Ivy League schools, especially the top four schools, almost entirely come from wealthy families and under the "legacy" admissions policy. Wealthy families know that the test scores are a game and that they can pay their way into that game through high-priced tutors who help their students get high test scores regardless of their grades. Wealthy families also know the other parts of the game that you don't, and even if you did, it is unlikely you can participate in because they have high barriers to entry. Wealthy families make contributions to the elite schools, and admissions departments receive calls from the president to stamp *accepted* onto many applications from wealthy families, regardless of the student's high school grades. Usually, that call comes when a student's performance doesn't warrant admission, but their family's connections are deemed *important* to the university.

A perfect example is Jared Kushner. Once a name not known outside of New York City real estate circles, as the former President's son-in-law and advisor, there has been a lot of research done into Jared's past that raised a lot of questions, like, how in the world did Jared get into Harvard? Well, it wasn't based on his grades or even his test scores. His father "gave"

Harvard $2.5 million the year before Jared graduated from high school, in installments of course, so he could leverage that *gift* and get his son accepted.

Jared's father, Charles Kushner, is a convicted criminal. He was convicted of tax violations, illegal campaign contributions, and retaliating against a witness, and spent two years in federal prison. But unlike Felicity Huffman, Jared's father will not go to jail for bribing his son's way into Harvard. Harvard's official story is that the contributions had nothing to do with his acceptance, although former officials at Jared's high school said his GPA and test scores did not warrant his acceptance. Old money has a different set of rules. Bribing a coach is unnecessary if you know the old money rules and contribute to the alumni fund, and you can call the school's president on his direct line.

Want more proof? Don't take my word for it; there are smarter people than me showing these disparities in detailed research. In her book *Pedigree,* Lauren Rivera takes you inside the world of firms that pay the extremely high salaries, the EPS firms mentioned earlier. These firms don't hire based on what you did in college; in fact, none of them trust the grading system at any of the universities. Instead, they hire based on who you were before you arrived at college. They may look at your extracurricular activities as a hiring consideration, and activities that are rich in elite social capital, like participation in lacrosse or rowing, are more ways that the wealthy continue to exclude everyone from their club. If everyone starts playing lacrosse, the unspoken requirements will shift to other activities that require a lot of money to participate and that only happen in exclusive clubs, such as polo.

You can't know what the wealthy rules are unless you are wealthy. The origin of the SAT has its roots in keeping everyone who isn't wealthy out of the Ivy League schools. The easiest way for the wealthy to keep their inner circle intact is to hide the requirements that keep the Ivy League school for the elite in plain sight. You don't have the test scores because you didn't learn the game of taking tests.

Enter the Khan Academy and the Asian students who adjust to the game and become great test-takers, thinking they will level the playing field, or so they thought. Instead, the courts have allowed the universities to limit the acceptance of Asian students despite their perfect GPAs and test scores. Why? Why wouldn't Harvard and Yale want the top students? Because they don't all come from wealthy families. Look at the acceptance rates of these elite universities, and things haven't changed at all, the wealthy continue to be accepted, just like Jared.

IVY LEAGUE TUITION IS AN AFTERTHOUGHT FOR THE WEALTHY:

Wealthy families have been paying private tuition for their children since grade school.

Ivy league tuition is almost the same. It's all a part of the old wealth rules.

Harvard initially won its lawsuit, allowing it to keep out more academically deserving Asian students under the guise of a "diverse student body." It took the Supreme Court to step in and eliminate skin color from university admissions. But this is unlikely to change anything. They also don't like to advertise that their "black" student population is not the African American students that you would think, it is often wealthy black families from around the world. Look at the actual number of students who are from lower-income families and it is less than 2%.

For the few, brilliant, ambitious students from lower-income families who do get into the Ivy League schools, you will still be different. You will be different simply because you are now around a lot of very, very wealthy people, and you are not part of their tribe, and it is not exactly an inviting group. When they fly off on private jets to private islands or spend the summer in unpaid internships that are not advertised, you'll feel left out. Work hard, get better grades to get yourself the job interviews with those EPS firms, and you will find you don't understand their interview format, aren't wearing the right clothes, and don't look like your interviewers... and then you realize why you didn't get that job. Old money around the world has been creating systems of inequality for centuries, why would today's college institutions be any different? I'd call myself a cynic if it all weren't true.

Takeaways in the Dirty Secrets They Don't Want You to Know

- Community college credit hours count the same, so they are equal value, and they usually are required to transfer by law.
- Class sizes at most universities for freshmen can be huge, and the diversity of a community college may actually provide a better learning experience.
- Most of us will end up with jobs that are not related to our degree.
- They cannot teach you everything you need to know, so don't give them all of your money and rights to your future earnings.
- No one pays sticker price, and admissions are often based on the student's family having the ability to pay, not that they deserve to be there. Most admissions offices won't admit it, but their problem is not that they don't have enough deserving students to let in, it's that they have to let in a lot of undeserving students who can afford to pay the high tuition price.
- Rankings are not important. They most likely mean that the school spends a lot of money on things other than professors that won't create value for your life but that you get to pay for in higher tuition.
- What you study can be more important than where you study. The labor market dictates wages.
- Associate degrees and certificates may be worth more than a bachelor's degree.

Part 5

The Real Cost of College

Questions on The Real Cost of College:

Question 22:

Have you heard of the student loan crisis? What kind of impact do you think this debt is having on the former students who took out these loans?

Question 23:

Do you know the definition of "opportunity cost"? What opportunity cost are you missing by going to school?

Question 24:

Do you plan on taking out any loans for college? Y/N

____

Question 24a.

If yes, how much? $__________________

Question 24b.

If yes to Q24, have you calculated the amount that you will have to earn to repay these loans, including interest and income taxes on the money earned? Y/N

Question 24c.

If yes to Q24a, how much do you calculate you will have to earn to repay the amount of debt you are taking out? $____________

Question 25:

Do you understand what "after-tax dollars" mean? Y/N

____

Question 26:

Suppose you could get a scholarship for $1,000 per semester. How much money would that save you from having to earn to repay a loan if you had borrowed the same $1,000? $__________________

Exploring the Real Cost of College

Currently, students owe over $1.5 trillion of student loans. This wasn't always the case. Twenty years ago, it was a few hundred million, most accrued by doctors, attorneys, and other graduate students. But tuition has increased over 500%, and room and board has increased as well. There are a lot of reasons for this, but that's not what this section is about. This section is about understanding the current cost of college and what you can do about it.

> **HOW MUCH WILL YOU GIVE AWAY?**
>
> How much of the additional lifetime value of college will you get?
>
> Total Additional Value: $550,000
>
> **Not to YOU:**
>
> » To the University: $100,000
> » Taxes 30%: $165,000
> » Interest: $ 60,000
> » Total to Others: $325,000
>
> **Total to You:** $225,000
>
> As much as half of the lifetime benefits of you attending college can go to others!

The current sticker price for most state universities is between $25,000 and $35,000 per year for tuition and room and board. That is a total of $100,000 or more to get a four-year degree! It's a staggering amount of money. The first question that this brings up is: *Is it worth it?* And the answer to that question used to be "yes," but through the years that changed to *"maybe,"* and now the honest answer for many students is *"probably not"*. Now, that answer may depend on the degree you will earn. The *"probably not"* answer is more from a practical standpoint of the lifetime benefits from going to college, versus the stress of dealing with student loans and the financial impact of debt. But we will try to look at this from several angles to help inform us.

According to Pew Research, the average lifetime earnings benefit (40 years of working) of going to college is approximately $550,000 (this has not been updated for inflation, but the lesson is the same – plug in your own estimate of additional earnings). However, when they calculated this benefit, they assumed that college would cost you roughly $5,000 in total. So, let's dig into where these extra earnings are going to end up. If you take out loans like Mary did, then a lot of that money earned could go to interest, but let's also not forget about good old Uncle Sam and taxes. If you have a nice Uncle named Sam, this is not that guy. This is the taxman who makes sure he gets a good chunk of your paycheck before you get the rest. Taxes are the only other guarantee in life besides death.

By getting your degree, you can expect to earn an extra $550,000, but before you get that money, Uncle Sam is going to take his part first. 7.5% will go to Social Security and Medicare taxes, and about 20% will go to federal income tax. Add in state taxes, and overall, total taxes on earnings are usually about 25-35% for most households. So, for sake of discussion, 30% goes to the taxman, leaving you with an extra $385,000 of actual earnings benefits from that college degree. But now you have to pay the school. If you pay them the $100,000 sticker price, that reduces your part of the additional earnings to $285,000.

Now, what if you had to borrow some of that $100,000 like Mary did? Interest expense will add up—in Mary's case to over $60,000, assuming she can make all her payments on time. We take out the interest cost, and we are down to $225,000 left for you. So, if we do that math again, 50% of the lifetime earnings benefit of going to college is **not** going to you, but to the university you choose to attend, the banks for interest, and the government for taxes.

We didn't take into account the stress of dealing with student loans, the potential impact of student loans on credit, and the impact of debt to allow you to buy a home or go have life experiences. In total, if you are borrowing, you could be giving 30% or more of your lifetime additional earnings to your university and banks. That ~~seems like~~ is a very high price.

Before we go any further in analyzing where you are giving away your efforts, let's get into the details of where the money goes for the cost of college. Typically, about half of the expense of college is for room and board—that's typically $50,000 over four years, if not more. Let's not forget, that is for group dormitory housing and the food equivalent of a lousy buffet for every meal. The remaining half goes to tuition. But as we have already discussed, we could reduce that tuition significantly by going to a community college first.

I want you to view the money you intend to spend on college as your cash pile and the benefit to your life. You have a lot of options to consider, but on average, your future benefit will be, after taxes, $385,000. Now you get to decide who you want to share this with and how much you want to give them. I'm under the assumption that you want that degree to have the university name on it so that you can access the alumni network.

First, I want you to remind you again that if you go to community college first, your degree does not come with an asterisk on it that says "only two years at university" or "community college transfer." It will only have the university name on it.

So how much of your money do you want to give to your university? If you borrow all the money and live on campus for four years and have $100k of student loans like Mary, you can give the university and banks over $160,000 of your money. Or, you could live at home and give them only $50,000. Or, you could go to community college first and give them only $30,000. And we can find even more ways to lower the cost further, if you are interested. It comes down to *how much time you are willing to spend*, just like our earlier example of buying a car. We both leave with the same thing, but our costs can be very different.

> **WHERE DOES THE MONEY GO?**
>
> About 50% of the cost of college is for room & board.

Let's move on to Q23: Opportunity cost. Opportunity cost is the money that you could have made if you just got a job instead of going to school. It is the money you are giving up by not working. For most young people, this isn't a huge number, but it is necessary to recognize that in addition to paying for school, you are also not working a full-time job. For many people who have to work a full-time job to help support their families, it's a leading reason they don't go to college. Just be aware that opportunity cost is real and that in addition to spending money on school, you are working limited, if any, hours, and that is lost revenue, also known as opportunity cost.

Next, we need to discuss the cost of money. If you are borrowing for school, the cost of money is significant. In Mary's case, we calculate it to be almost $60,000 of interest expense. When you consider this as a percentage of the additional amount Mary will earn after taxes of $385,000, it means that almost one out of every six dollars of Mary's additional earnings from going to school will go to a bank. If you have a job now and one out of every six additional dollars you earn went to pay a bank, you would not be happy. You need to know how much money you will have to pay the bank before you sign up for your loans. There is a reason they don't give you a lot of financial education. You are more likely just to sign

If you were offered a job for $300,000 per year to not go to college next year, would you take it?

You would be crazy not to.

Paying out-of-state tuition is like turning down a $300,000 per year job because that is equivocally the amount you will pay extra if you borrow out-of-state tuition.

the forms and not think of other ways to get the degree you want without the debt.

If you convert this entire discussion into days worked, would you agree to work one five days for the next 20 years to pay for a degree, pay more in taxes and pay a bank interest for your college debt?

Hopefully, the examples above have shown you the impact of taxes and interest that you will have to pay if you take out loans. Now, let's transition and start discussing additional ways you can limit how much you are spending on your degree.

The first is Federal Student Aid. Typically to be eligible, you have to come from a low-income family. Now some recent scandals in Illinois involved people who tried to get around this by changing guardianship of students. Since this is not illegal, if it gets you more financial aid, go for it! I'm sure they will close this loophole, but if it is not illegal, then use it while it is available.

Out-of-State Tuition: The Worst Value of All

There is one particular part of paying for college that makes the least amount of sense: out-of-state tuition. There is no value to this expense, but universities love it as a way to boost income. Schools charge as much as $30,000 per year in "nonresident supplemental tuition." Simply put, it is a fee they can charge, so they do, to as many students as they can.

The University of Oregon boasts the highest percentage of out-of-state students at over 46% of their student body. They spend a lot of money on marketing to increase their student body, specifically out-of-state students. The goal is financial: Out-of-state students at Oregon pay annual tuition of $34,600 versus an in-state amount of $11,500. Adding 3,000 more students who each pay an extra $23k/year equates to an additional $69 million per year.

Simply put, out-of-state tuition is a complete waste of money. If you have to borrow this money and pay interest over the life of a loan, you will need to earn upwards of $300,000 in the future just to cover the out-of-state portion. What if I offered you a $300,000/year job as an 18-year-old, and all you had to do was move to the state where you wanted to attend school? You would take that offer immediately. Not moving and waiting to go to school is the equivalent of turning down this job. Simply put, out-of-state tuition is money wasted.

Now, if you really want to go to an out-of-state school, there are some smarter ways to go about it. It is not my recommendation because you lose the ability to live at home which can account for half the cost of school, but if you have to go out of state, or you are part of the 50% of students from New Jersey who choose to go out of state for school, then there are some practical options for you in Supplement 4.

Scholarships are worth almost three times their face value, versus borrowing.

Why? Because
When you borrow, you have to earn, then pay taxes, then pay interest and then repay the loan.

Know the value of a scholarship and make it your job to find as many scholarships as you can.

The Value of Scholarships and Grants

As part of the Federal Student Aid application process, there are several forms you need to fill out. Many of these forms are to determine eligibility for scholarships.

Question 26 discusses the value of scholarships. I ask this to get you familiar with how much money scholarships can save you in future costs. As in Mary's case, when you are borrowing money and must repay that money after taxes and with interest, *scholarships are worth almost three times face value.* That's right, the answer to Q26 is that a $1,000 scholarship will save Mary nearly $3,000. The point of this exercise is to change your perception of how much scholarships are worth and get you to treat scholarship applications as a part-time job. They are worth 3X, so don't think the $500 scholarship is not worth pursuing. Put into context, if you end up making $30/hour in your job after college, that $500 scholarship is worth 50 hours of work. Use apps such as Scholly to try to find more opportunities to reduce your costs with scholarships.

Grants work the same as scholarships. The most commonly known is the Federal Pell Grant, but most states also offer similar types of gifts, typically called governor's grants, or Colorado (replace your state name here) College Grants. Usually, if you are eligible for these grants, you also qualify for work-study. Federal Pell Grants are your money (unlike loans), so if you find ways to get other forms of tuition reimbursement, like through an employer who pays tuition reimbursement, then they will give you the additional money. State grants don't always work this way, but we will discuss how you can use the Federal Pell Grant to optimize your plan to graduate debt-free.

Takeaways in the Real Cost of College

- You are giving away a lot of your future earning benefits if you pay sticker price, or even the discounted price, for college and even more of your future if you take out loans.
- You can spend a lot of your future benefits by paying for housing. If you have the opportunity to live at home, it may not be ideal at 18, but it may be better than moving back home at age 22 because you have given away so much of your future earnings to pay for room and board.
- You will have to pay taxes on your future earnings, so calculate the future benefits to you by knowing the cost of tuition and the cost of interest on your loans.
- Scholarships and grants count 3X, so make your new part-time job applying for all the scholarships, federal (automatic with your FAFSA form), and state grants that you can.

PART 6

Family Finances

Question 27:

What is your family's ability to help you with education expenses?

Question 28:

Can you live at home? Y/N

Question 29:

As a thought exercise, would the family's money be better off invested in the stock market or other assets than paying for tuition?

When it comes to family finances and paying for college, there is no right answer for what a family should or should not be able to pay. Your experience may vary from your peers': your family might not discuss costs at all, or your family might agree to pay for everything with or without a discussion, or your parents may sit down with you and discuss their ability to pay in great detail.

While financial discussions are often emotionally uncomfortable because we are not taught to discuss finance, they are critical in order not to make the wrong choice about education and debt.

Is it better to live at home while going to college, or move back in after school and be saddled with debt?

The first thing that we need to discuss is how parents may not be rational regarding their children. Biologically, when a child is born, most parents instantaneously become selfless, willing to walk into traffic for their children and do anything for their survival. This instinct is a natural part of life, and it ensures the species will continue. While it might not happen to all parents, it happens to most. The implication is that we need to be aware of our emotions because emotions alone can lead to poor decision-making when it comes to paying for college, and especially when taking on debt. Often, it is parents or even grandparents who sign on for enormous loans so their children can go to college.

I wrote a blog post on my website, www.keepyours.org as a plea to parents to "start acting like adults" and help limit their children from taking on too much student loan debt. That conversation needs to extend to the parents themselves. Stop taking out debt yourself for your children. Parents, you have a choice! While it may seem to go against that natural desire to be selfless, it's a burden to your children and your family to take on massive amounts of debt.

Discussing family finances may be difficult, but it is critical to avoiding the wrong choices around debt and education.

This topic is a necessary conversation between parents and children. I don't believe many children want to see their parents carrying the debt for their education, nor do I think parents want their children struggling with debt after college, especially since the primary motive for students to go to college is to improve not just their own lives, but the lives of their family. We are in a crisis, and it is so bad that retired people are having their social security checks garnished for student loan debts, many of which they took out for their children. This burden puts parents in need of more help from their children, precisely the opposite position everyone was hoping to achieve by obtaining a college degree.

You, the student, must have honest conversations with your family about their ability to help you with college expenses. The reason we ask Question 28 is that if you can live at home, even if it is not ideal, you can see how much money that can save you. We discussed in the last section that room and board comprise almost half the cost of a college degree. So, if you can live at home now, that's a 50% contribution from your family! Parents, you can feel great about your ability to contribute if you can just provide housing.

I know that as an 18-year-old, staying at home does not sound like a fun plan. You're ready to be independent, have life experiences, and the freedom to do as you please, not have Mom and Dad around to tell you what to do anymore. Mom and Dad are likely ready for a break too! But ask yourself this question: Would you rather live at home now while you go to school, or move back in at 22 when you graduate because you are broke due to your student loan payments? So, how do we make this work?

I suggest a contract between parents and their college-age children. You're in college, so you are supposed to be a young adult. This means you will have certain additional responsibilities but also be given additional freedoms. The contract can be a tool to help everyone agree on how things will be. There are likely to be hot topics, and parents usually like to defer to the "My house, my rules" stance, but if we treat housing as paying for college, then it's the equivalent of your child paying rent, and they need to be treated more like a roommate. So, the contract usually goes something like this:

1. No rent charged, as long as grades are above a 2.5 GPA. Other costs parents can help with and agree to pay so long as grades are up: cell phone, car insurance, etc.
2. The student agrees to go to all their classes except when sick. (Student, you are paying for them, so why wouldn't you go?)

3. If you are going to be out past 11 PM (or some other agreed upon time), text or call.
4. Students don't have to say where they were if they go out with friends and stay over. They just have to notify them they will not be coming home before 11 PM.
5. Chores the student will do as part of room and board: cleaning, dishes, shopping, etc.
6. Any other points of contention – get them out in the open and agreed upon beforehand.

If you are a practical student and going to live at home and hopefully take the advice here and go to community college first, then you can skip this section, but for families who can afford to send their kids to college and pay full price, or for those families considering taking on lots of student loans or spending all four years at a university, this thought experiment be worth considering.

Alternative Use of Family Money

Thought Exercise: What if, instead of sending your child to school, the family invested the money saved for the college fund?

I have a friend who is very well off, and even if he was unwilling to pay for any school his kid wanted to go to, I'm positive the grandparents would pick up the tab. When we last discussed this, his daughter was applying to small liberal arts schools where the average tuition with room and board was almost $60,000 per year—about the same as out-of-state at UCLA. So, I asked him if her attending would be worth it, from a *"family money"* perspective. I also asked him not to take that personally because, of course, he would walk into traffic for his daughter, so naturally, he would pay for college because he can afford it. If you have the money, spending it on school can feel mandatory as a parent, but the premise here is to discuss value and family money.

I raise this question strictly to discuss value and as a thought experiment. Is that Honda Accord-level degree worth $240,000 (Maserati prices), when you could live at home and get the same degree for $50,000 or less? And sometimes the parents answer (especially if they can afford it), YES! Sometimes parents are also ready for the kids to be gone so they can get on with their new lives (don't tell the kids).

Let's try to take all of the emotion out of this thought experiment and just look at it from the additional lifetime earnings versus the cost. This takes more of a family business approach: "Should we invest in this opportunity, which will cost $100,000 and give us back $550,000 over the next 40 years, or should we invest that money in the stock market or other assets?" If we invest it in the stock market and get a 7% return, then in 40 years, we would have $1,796,934 (both numbers are before any taxes).

So, from strictly an investment perspective, the $100,000 for a degree that will earn you an additional $550,000 in lifetime earnings doesn't seem like the smart move for family money. Again, I can already hear the parents who think this is a crazy discussion and would want to yell at me about how this is about more than money; it is about a child's life, a child who they would do anything for. Please know that I am a college graduate and that this exercise is not about all those things. It is strictly a thought experiment to show the potential difference in value, largely due to the massive increasing in tuition. It is a value proposition discussion. What is best for the family?

Every student needs to understand their family's financial situation, and it should not be an "all or nothing" discussion. Instead, it's a thought experiment on value, and the math informs us that it is a better investment to spend the money on tuition rather than the stock market when the cost is about $39,000 or less. So, from a value proposition perspective, spending more than $39,000 for a college degree is likely not to pay off for the family in the long run versus investing that money for the family. This equation gives us a solid idea of what college costs should stay under, and an assessment of the long-term value for the family of a degree.

Has anyone taken a tour of the university and been told that if you pay more than $39,000, then it may be wiser just to invest the money instead? While many parents have had to think through the value dilemma, this simply shows the math to help foster the discussion. As a parent, you could show your child the math and investment option that instead of giving them the $39,000 to go to school, you are going to invest that money and provide them with the total investment amount later in life. Why should they spend all their time earning that money when the money you have now could work for them without any additional effort of attending college?

More importantly, this thought exercise can provide valuable information when we discuss the different paths we could take on the way to getting that college degree. If the money is available, maybe it would be wiser to not spend it all on room and board and tuition, perhaps some of it we should save as the beginning nest egg.

What if my friend showed this math to his daughter and said to her that he was willing to spend all the $240,000 on her education if she wanted, but that after college, she was on her own? But if she wanted to, instead of spending all that money, she could choose the other path to live at home, go to community college and then to the local university and when she graduated, she could have the difference. What if she took that opportunity and spent only $40,000 for her degree, and now had $200,000 to start her life with after school to buy a home or invest early in life? How much more would she learn investing that money than she would learn in school?

Now my friend's case is not the reason I've included this topic. He has more than enough money to cover the tuition, but I know a lot of middle-class families who spend a lot of their family wealth on education. A lot of families are paying the $100,000+ sticker price for four years of tuition and room and board at the state university, not thinking about what they will have left over when it's done. Worse, many families don't have the money and are taking out loans that leave students and their parents with decades of debt for education. For many families, this means that parents are not funding their retirement, paying off their home, or foregoing other investment opportunities so they can pay for high tuition rates.

Most students can hardly comprehend how much money their parents are spending because these are after tax dollars. Remember Uncle Sam, the taxman? He already took his cut of that money, so it is likely your parents had to earn close to $200,000 to have the money to pay for your $100,000 education. I don't think many (if any) parents sit down with their children and offer them this type of mixed scenario, where instead of spending a large part of the family's wealth, they offer the child the opportunity to do college in a thriftier manner and still get the same degree.

I hope this thought experiment encourages the conversation about family money, parents' retirement, and how much their children may have to help them if all the family money gets spent on school. Understand the value proposition and what alternatives may look like. It is almost impossible to understand the difficulty of earning these large sums of money for anyone who's not in the workforce.

Takeaways in Family Finances

- If you can live at home, that can reduce your college expenses by about half. Parents, if all you have to contribute is room and board, don't discount providing accommodation, it has a lot of value.
- Know the family budget for college help. Not discussing it in detail can lead to many bad decisions, and no family members want to see others in deep debt.
- Know the value of a degree and acknowledge that family money may not be best spent on an expensive college degree with high costs for room and board. Once costs exceed a total of $40,000, the family may be better off investing the money instead.
- Be open to ideas to get thrifty on the educational expenses to have available family money after graduation as a nest egg to start your career.

Stories of Family Finances

Once in a while, I start the discussion of college and debt with someone new and get a story that everyone should hear. This past year I had such a conversation with Matt (named changed to protect the innocent). I've played basketball with Matt's father for over 15 years, and Matt now plays with us, having returned from college. Matt worked during his summers in high school and college selling windows door-to-door.

Matt's effort selling windows gives a view into the effort required to get through college debt-free. Selling door-to-door is simply a numbers game: If one out of 50 doors knocked on turns into a customer buying, you need to knock on 50 doors to get the next sale; therefore, the strategy is how to knock on as many doors as you can? Matt's approach was to sprint between houses. His friends laughed at him as they took cigarette breaks and strolled between houses, but Matt's sprinting was rewarded, as he outsold his friends every month, just through the effort of knocking on more doors. Matt also saved his money made during his junior and senior years of high school for his college expenses. Matt went to BYU, a very affordable, private school in Provo, Utah, which also has low housing costs.

Matt was able to cover all of his expenses while in college with his savings from his summer job and graduated with no debt. While waiting for his job to start after college, he went back to selling windows for one final summer and made enough to save for a 3.5% down payment on a home. He started his new job, bought a house, and filled it with roommates. He now pays under $100 a month in rent after collecting rent from all the roommates, so he has the lowest rent cost of all of his friends, and he can invest the difference. Meanwhile, the roommates are paying for the home! Matt has no debt and is building his wealth, but what about the roommates? They are all in debt from college and buying his house for him.

You can get through school debt-free. Matt's story is not 20 years old; he graduated recently. Matt had a plan, and he is not asking for debt forgiveness from a political candidate or worried about how to pay back his mountain of student loan debt. It causes him no stress and he doesn't have to think about if his degree was worth it. Matt is learning more about how to invest and grow his money and taking advantage of opportunities from not being in debt.

What situation do you want to be in when you graduate from college? Put that into your plan!

PART 7

Hacking the System

Question 30:

Do you believe it is possible to get the degree you want without taking out student loan debt? Y/N

___

___

Question 31:

Are you willing to work while you go to college? Y/N

___

Question 32:

Do you have a goal for how little debt you want to take out?

Amount: $___

Question 33:

Do you want a degree from a specific school? What school and why?

___

___

When I first started researching student loan debt, my inner "hustle" voice immediately asked, "Could I get the degree I wanted right now, from the premier state school, without going into any debt?" After calculating total costs (including what I would save by living at home), researching companies that offer tuition reimbursement, and including job income I could have while in school, it became apparent that yes, I could get a degree without debt, but not without substantial effort. Just like Matt running door to door.

After I did the first Keep Yours podcast on how to graduate with no debt (see my Student Loan series on the site), someone came to me and asked, "That sounds nice, but I live in a rural community, so there is no community college nearby, and my family doesn't have the means to support me. Do you have a plan for me?" I always want to say yes and believe there is a path if there is a desire to get there. However, without factoring in a Federal Pell Grant, if you still want to go to the premier state school, the answer became more of a "maybe", which I didn't like. However, that is an honest answer and shows how ~~complicated~~ broken the system is right now with tuition costs increasing as much as they have in the past 20 years.

If you want to go to a private liberal arts school where sticker price tuition is often over $50,000 per year, the answer is "no." Unless your parents have a considerable budget for you, there is no way you escape those expenses without a lot of debt. But, all of these questions take us back to the value proposition, the reason for the degree, and the expected additional lifetime earnings.

As I've said before, if your grades and test scores are that good, if you're that smart and ambitious, if you can get accepted into an Ivy League school, the people you will meet and the opportunities available are likely worth the cost, despite the debt.

However, I also know people who have graduated from Ivy League schools and their parents would have been better off investing the money because they lack the ambition to do anything with that knowledge and opportunity. Having gone to a smaller school and having discussed this topic with people from all walks of life, the importance of where you went to school will not matter in the long term. It is what you do while you are on campus, and what you do after graduation that will truly matter. You may have to work a little harder, you may not have as large of an alumni group to lean on, and it may be harder getting that first job. But the freedom you will have from not having a big, burdensome pile of debt bricks in your backpack is easily worth those extra efforts during college.

For most of us, we just want to get a good education and have future opportunities. If you are ambitious and want to hack the system, you can, and here are some strategies to do it regardless of your family's ability to help you and whether or not you qualify for Federal Pell Grants.

No Debt Plan 1 – For Those Who Can Live at Home

The first plan is very straight forward: get a premier state school degree while you live at home. Work at UPS or another company with tuition reimbursement. I will use UPS as the example here, but many companies now offer tuition reimbursement. UPS has an excellent tuition reimbursement plan and pays a decent hourly wage. For your first two years, attend a community college, preferably one with a direct transfer program. The example I gave earlier of Red Rocks Community College with their direct program to the University of Colorado engineering program is a perfect example. Freshman and sophomore tuition would be covered under the employee reimbursement plan, and hopefully you can save most of your earnings from the job while living at home. The final two years you attend the premier state school (University of Colorado as an example), with the first $5,250 of tuition covered by tuition reimbursement and the remainder paid through savings and wages from working.

This plan will not be easy, but it is a good combination of work and academia, which will give you the motivation to go to class, so you don't have to keep moving boxes for the rest of your life. Take it from someone who worked on a farm during college summers, having a difficult manual labor job is great motivation to get good grades so you are not at that same job in 20 years. Having a job that gives you physical exercise can also help you focus when in class. Living at home may not be ideal, but if you can graduate with a degree and no debt, then you will have a fantastic time in your 20's and 30's, having money to spend on experiences or investments, while those who chose to take out debt do not have that option.

While we can all acknowledge that working through college is difficult and we might prefer not to work and have more time for social engagements, I can promise you that if you choose to work during college to significantly reduce your debts, your future self will certainly thank you for it, especially if you can find an employer with tuition reimbursement!

Sometimes I hear from students that do not have enough time to have a job and go to school. I counter that argument with the fact that I had a job, played basketball on the school team which required as much time or more than a job, and went to school full time. I know a lot of people who worked through school, you can too.

No Debt Plan 2 – For Those Who Cannot Live at Home

Now suppose you can't live at home and have no family support. It will be challenging to graduate from the same premier state school debt-free without taking some other measures, such as going into the military first and using the GI Bill after honorable discharge. Another option is to attend a smaller state school in a place with a lower cost of living (this is what I did). Another idea could be to move to Louisville, Kentucky, where, if you are willing to work the night shift, UPS will pay for all of your educational expenses, and you can use your earnings for room and board.

If your family cannot provide you any support, then hopefully you qualify for Federal Financial Aid. That is about $5,000 per year and will help, but if you are determined to get through college with no debt, school choice will still be an issue. An engineering or similar high paying degree with a small amount of debt could also be the right answer. If you can get other scholarships, it is possible to graduate with no debt and still attend the premier state school.

If you are eligible for federal aid and you can get the $5,000 per year, and you can live at home at least for two years while at community college, then the math gets much better for you. If your employer covers your community college tuition, you can bank the federal grant money from your freshman and sophomore years and use it for your junior and senior years to help cover the costs of tuition and/or housing. If we do the calculations again for the University of Colorado for two years, including room and board, it is possible to graduate with no debt.

The math looks like this: For the first two years at community college, tuition is covered by UPS, savings from the job are about \$10K/year plus the additional \$5K/year in federal grants, equaling a total savings of \$30K at the end of sophomore year. Year 3, \$5K in grant money, \$5K from UPS, and \$7K in wages against \$30k in tuition and room and board expenses = \$13k of savings used, \$17k of savings remaining. Repeat for year 4 = degree with no debt.

As we discussed in Chapter 2, knowing the salary for your desired job is important in making your decision of where to go to school and assessing the value proposition of the costs and debt you are willing to take on. If you want to be a teacher, then a degree from a smaller state school that is much less expensive is a wiser choice than going to the more expensive premier state school. The value proposition makes more sense. A lot of students realize this and go to smaller state colleges and that allows them to not be burdened by higher student loan payments in jobs with lower salaries. Remember, your college experience is more about what you do on campus than which campus you are on even though schools want you to believe the opposite.

Creating a budget for where you want to be with debt after school is essential and will help you develop boundaries before you start looking at offers and deciding where to attend. If you don't have boundaries, then the salespeople at the universities will exploit your dreams and drown you in debt that they call “aid”. Please don’t let that happen, it can destroy your future.

Employers with Tuition Reimbursement:

This is not intended to be a complete list, but examples of companies that can help you get through college without debt.

a) Amazon: up to $12,000 over 4 years
b) UPS – up to $25,000 and a maximum of $5,250 per year.
c) Chipotle – up to $5,250 per year.
d) Starbucks – all of it – if you can get into Arizona State online
e) McDonald's - $2,500 per year
f) Taco Bell/Pizza Hut - $5,250
g) Home Depot – part-time - $1,500 per year, more for full time and salaried employees
h) Publix - $3,200 per year, maximum of $12,800
i) Verizon - $4,000 per year
j) United Health Group
k) Best Buy
l) Sam's Club

The Value of Tuition Reimbursement

Just as we discussed the value of scholarships, the value of tuition reimbursement is 2.65X the face amount if you would otherwise have to take out loans. Remember, you would have to work to earn that money, then pay taxes, and pay interest on the loan. So, for each year that you get $5,250 from UPS or another employer, the value of that versus taking out loans is $13,885 per year (see side chart with 7% interest rate and 20-year term). That's the equivalent of UPS paying you an additional $7 per hour or more, depending on how many hours you work. We often underestimate the value of tuition reimbursement because of the dollar amount, not understanding the form (before you pay taxes or after) of payment and the cost of interest.

Housing Hacks

For those who just can't handle living at home, there is a potential housing hack – become a Resident Assistant. You won't be able to do this your freshman year, and it typically requires that you take a class on it during your first year, but if you are set on going to a four-year university immediately and you don't want to live at home, this could be a hack for you. However, you need a contingency plan. Taking this on as a plan still requires you to have the room and board, typically about $15,000 a year, for the first year. But if you don't mind helping babysit the dorm, then this could work for you.

This strategy may work best for students who are eligible for Federal Pell Grants and governor's grants and choose a smaller state school. If your Governor's Grant covers a large part of your tuition and your Federal Pell Grant and work-study can cover your room and board your first year, then this hack could be perfect for you (Federal Pell Grant is only $6,000/year, but room and board at smaller schools is typically much less than the large state schools).

If you keep up your grades so you continue to receive the Governor's Grant for tuition, and your sophomore year you work as a Resident Assistant which covers your room and board, you could graduate with money in the bank, as they will give you cash if your expenses do not exceed your Federal Pell Grant. I know this because many of my friends and teammates were eligible for Federal Pell Grants. When those exceeded what they owed in tuition (since many were on scholarships or partial scholarships), they received the difference.

Loans, Earnings and Taxes

If you took out a $5,250 loan to repay that loan would look like this:

Debt: $5,250

Interest Rate: 7%

Number of Year to repay: 20

Monthly Payment: $41

Total of all Payments: $9,769

But to pay, first you must earn and pay taxes on those earnings.

At 30% in total taxes

(7.65% Social Security, 17% Federal and 5% State, total of 30%)

Earnings Needed: $13,866

Your employer paying you $5,250 in tuition is really like them paying you $13,866 in wages.

Look at the math another way:

Earnings:	$13,866
Taxes:	$4,117
Funds Available:	$9,769
Interest Expense:	$4,519
Principal Paid	$5,250

This hack doesn't work as well at the large state schools because you have the high cost of room and board and high-cost tuition, so it is unlikely that all the grants will cover tuition, but if you can work as an RA instead of borrowing that money, that's a great hack!

But don't bet on it. You won't have control over whether or not you get the job, so you'll need a backup plan. At a smaller school with lower costs that is easier to do. At large state schools, if you don't get the RA job and live in the dorm again for a second year, that could take $15,000 out of your budget. If this sounds like an interesting plan for you, make sure you have a backup plan with an employer that has tuition reimbursement.

There is another housing hack that is similar in being a part time job and that is becoming a property manager for a large apartment complex. While a 19 year is not exactly the perfect person for a landlord to trust, if you have had other jobs and are handy at fixing things or good with people, then this is a job that often is paid in free rent. It is also an opportunity to learn about property management and the business of real estate.

Federal Student Aid – Pell Grant Help

For low-income families, the Federal Financial Aid system does offer some help. While the amount of a Federal Pell Grant has not risen with the increase in the costs of college, it can still be a great benefit, and when used correctly, keep you from taking on debt. However, as I saw firsthand, it is much easier for recipients to spend that money on a better wardrobe, partying, and other niceties than to save it for tuition expenses. The maximum Pell Grant award for 2019-2020 was $6,195, and you are eligible to receive this amount for up to six years. That is a total lifetime benefit potential of $37,170 and a four-year benefit of almost $25,000.

If we look at how we could use that $25,000 to stay out of debt and we can combine that money with a job (including work-study), employer tuition reimbursement, etc., getting through college with no loans can get a little easier. But we can also fall into the trap of deciding that the Federal Pell grant will reduce tuition enough that we don't want to work, so we forego the tuition reimbursement money from a job and end up at the exact same place, taking out debt to cover the difference. But what if you get really smart with this money?

> **Pell Grant Hack:**
>
> **Live at home and go to community college and save your Pell Grant money for the last two years of tuition at a four-year university**

What if you still go to community college first? The community college tuition should be much less than the $6,000 Pell Grant, but instead of spending the extra money, like most of us would do, what if you saved it instead? This would allow you to put that money towards tuition when you transfer to the university, and reduce the amount you owe. If you have a job as well, that may mean you now have extra money to help pay for a car and other expenses while you go to school. If you are eligible for a Pell Grant, you will likely qualify for additional tuition assistance from the state to pay for your community college tuition.

If you are eligible, use that Pell Grant money wisely. When I was in community college, I saw many of my classmates spend their Pell Grant money on clothes and video games. They treated it as though it was a birthday gift instead of their future tuition money. If you are eligible, a Federal Pell Grant is a gift, but one you should use wisely (and I realize that is a very tough concept at 18-years old).

Takeaways on Hacking the System:

- It is possible to get through college with no debt.
- If you have no family support, you will likely need to work and find an employer with tuition reimbursement to graduate from the top state universities with minimal debt.
- The value proposition of private liberal arts schools is not very good. For families who can comfortably afford it, that money could alternatively be invested with higher returns then the average increase in lifetime wages from getting a degree. For families going into debt, there is a point at which you will be giving up all of the increase in your earnings and dealing with the stress of debt for life.
- Know the burden of debt and have a goal of zero or a small amount and plan accordingly.
- Find companies with tuition reimbursement programs.
- If you are eligible for a Federal Pell Grant, use that money wisely as part of your overall plan to stay out of debt. Save it while you go to community college to cover the higher tuition cost when you transfer to a university.
- In the right situation, being an RA could save you a lot in room and board, but don't bet on getting the job.

PART 8

Four Choices, Four Lives

"A smart person learns from their mistakes; a wise person will learn from the mistakes of others." I'm not sure whom to attribute that quote to, but I know it is hard for all of us to learn from others' mistakes and not have to repeat those ourselves to get the lessons. Our choices have consequences, and the more dire those consequences are, the more we should strive to learn vicariously from others. Hopefully, you have learned about the long-term impact of student debt. To illustrate the impact, this chapter will focus on four different students' choices and approaches to debt and the long term outcomes from the effects of those choices.

Meet Billy, Shanice, Sofia, and Jalen. All four of them want to graduate from the University of Colorado in Boulder, all want degrees in engineering. They all have different stories and will make different decisions, and those decisions will have long term impacts on their lives.

Billy is from Flint, Michigan. He has enjoyed making things since he was young. He doesn't want to stay in Michigan—the winters are too long and too cold and he has seen the ups and downs of his father's career working for the big auto companies that have now abandoned Flint. Billy wants to make things that change people's lives and has always felt like a leader in his classes. He thinks he could run his own engineering firm one day. Billy applied to several schools, but Colorado was on the top of his list, and he was extremely excited when he was accepted. His aunt lives in Broomfield and will allow Billy to stay in the room in her basement if Billy stays in school and helps around the house.

Shanice is from Longmont, Colorado. Her mother, Alice, is an engineer at a Colorado-based company that makes medical instruments. Shanice can see the products that her mom works on, and that makes it easy for her to see how those products save lives and make people's lives better. Shanice has done well in school and was excited to get the acceptance letter from the University of Colorado. Many of her friends are going there immediately, and she feels pressured to go with them.

Our four heroes, and the impact of their choices:

BILLY
SHANICE
SOFIA
JALEN

Sofia is from Denver, Colorado. Sofia has attended many football games at the university with her father, who is a CU graduate. Since she was a freshman in high school, Sofia has had her mind made up that CU is where she wants to attend. Many of Sofia's friends will be attending CU, and she is excited to leave home and experience "college life."

Jalen is from Broomfield, Colorado. He has a neighbor, John, who is an engineer, and he loves helping him with projects and wants to be an engineer to make things, too. Jalen worked especially hard as a sophomore and junior in high school to improve his test scores and GPA for his application to CU. He recently got the acceptance letter and was very excited to share it with John.

It would be challenging to find four students who want to pursue the same degree and have the exact same financial resources. However, to illustrate the impact of the decision making, all four students will have no family financial resources to help pay tuition. Yet, they all have the option to live at home or with a family member while attending school. Billy has the unique decision of deciding whether to take a gap year or pay out-of-state tuition.

All four students visited the University of Colorado campus and toured the engineering facilities. They were impressed by the robotics labs, applied science classrooms, and learning spaces they would have access to as engineering students. The admissions counselors instructed all of them that they were lucky to have been accepted to the engineering program and should enroll as freshmen to ensure they keep their spots in the program. None of the counselors discussed the pathway programs the university offers for community college students despite their website saying that 25% of CU engineering graduates come from community college transfer students.

The Students' Choices

Billy was so ecstatic when he received his admission acceptance letter that he didn't even bother to look at the costs. His mother asked him a few questions, but how could she not support his enthusiasm? Being able to tell all of his classmates that he was headed for Colorado and seeing the jealousy on some of their faces made Billy all the more convinced he had made the right decision. "Yeah, it was going to cost a lot, but an engineering degree would mean big money down the line, it's one of the highest paying degrees," Billy told his classmates. Billy didn't see any way this could be a wrong decision.

Shanice was equally excited to see her acceptance letter come in the mail. While she knew her mother's influence had given her an advantage in school, she was still worried she might not get in. She sat down with the letter and her mother to discuss the decision. When her mother suggested she live at home, Shanice was not happy. So many of her friends would be living on campus, and she wanted to have that experience with them. "How could you not want me to have that experience?" she screamed at her mother as she stormed out of the room.

Shanice's mother, Alice, being the engineer that she was, sat down and reviewed all of the costs for school. She was divorced and much of her salary went to pay for their home. She also didn't have much saved for Shanice for college. She knew that if she was going to help Shanice with school, it could come from her living at home. Or, she could sell the house, get an apartment, and give the difference to Shanice. Alice had put herself through school and had only recently paid off her student loans, and she didn't want Shanice to have the same financial struggles that she had faced because of school debt. Finally, Shanice and Alice sat down again to review the costs and make a decision. Alice went over the total expenses for school, the different options, how she could help, and why she didn't want Shanice to go into debt. Finally, Alice told Shanice that she would support her the best she could with her decision, but Alice was not willing to take out more debt for her daughter, as she had just paid off her own student loans.

It took several weeks before Shanice wanted to tell any of her friends her decision. She couldn't ask her mother to sell the house, and she knew her mom was right about living with all the debt. Shanice knew they almost lost the house after the divorce because her mom was still paying off student loans. It was her mom's final question to her that had been bothering her the most. Alice asked, "If your friend goes through the community college gateway program and pays less in tuition than you do, why is the degree worth the extra money it costs to go to CU for all four years?" Shanice had no answer; she knew the answer was that there was no extra value. She wanted the experience to be with her friends, to not have to tell them that while she got accepted, she was going to live at home and go to community college for two years first before going to CU. She felt embarrassed that her family finances didn't allow for the full experience, and like all the hard work she had put into high school and getting a good SAT score was for nothing.

Alice was very proud of Shanice's decision. She knew her daughter was conflicted and wanted the college experience that she and her friends had dreamed about and planned. She also agreed that they would have a different set of house rules and that Shanice could spend time with her friends and stay the night in the dorms with them so she wouldn't miss out on completely on the college social experience.

Sofia's decision was much easier. It was what she had always wanted, and her father could see her excitement and agreed to support her with whatever loans she needed. It was what everyone said you should do, and they both figured the degree and additional earnings would repay the debt she would need to take on. Sofia's father wanted her to have the same college experience he had, so with little discussion, the family accepted that Sofia would spend all four years at the university, despite the costs.

Jalen rushed over to his neighbor John's house with his acceptance letter. To Jalen, it was almost a dream that he had turned into a reality. Was he really going to be able to make things? It was overwhelming, and they celebrated the accomplishment. Then, about a week later, John started asking Jalen questions about paying for school and the amount of debt Jalen would need. At first, Jalen just thought it would be worth it, no matter the amount of debt, to improve his family's situation. Jalen's mom had recently remarried, and Jalen looked forward to the day that he could help his mom with the family finances. John had paid his way through college at a smaller state school and had seen the impact of student loan debts on his co-workers as they tried to start families. He didn't want to put a damper on Jalen's excitement and dreams, but knew it was important to share his experiences. John researched options for Jalen, found a small community that was trying to help students get through school without any debt, and turned it into a game for Jalen by asking him questions. John walked Jalen through the engineering process for his decisions, which Jalen viewed as his first thing to make himself.

John asked lots of questions, and the "why" and "what" were easy to answer: The simple answer to why he wanted to go to college was to improve his family's life and get a good career. The next question was, "How do you get there?" John used Jalen's previous hard work to show him that this was the important part, how hard he worked at it and having a passion for it. John's questions continued: Do they have different books? No. Do the community college course credits count that same? Yes. Then why pay the extra money for the first two years? Jalen started seeing the bigger picture that John was creating for him. This was just a game and after seeing the math on student loan debt, Jalen could see that debt would take a lot of his hard work to pay off and he would be paying a lot of interest to banks.

John and Jalen researched together to come up with the best possible plan. Jalen planned on working through school, but it hadn't occurred to him to try to get a job with a company that pays tuition reimbursement. It is not something you consider in high school when you're just trying to make some extra money and get accepted by schools.

Jalen finally settled on UPS because they had flexible shifts and would work with him while he was going to school. He found the right transfer program through Front Range Community College and applied to UPS before he graduated high school. Because of his research and talking to a few UPS drivers, Jalen knew that UPS hired temporary workers in the summer to cover their full-time employees' vacations. If you did a good job, they would keep you on full time, and then you would be eligible for tuition reimbursement.

John was shocked by Jalen's decisions; Jalen had developed a much better plan than he had hoped to get through school, but John knew it was also going to be a tough four years for Jalen. He used some of the goal-setting tools he had learned along the way to help Jalen break down the goal of a degree into several parts, so he could have small accomplishments along the way.

They decided to take it year by year:

» Year one goal: Get the UPS job and knock out all of the basic courses at the community college.
» Year two: Finish his associate's degree and get accepted back into the CU program. Worry about the next two years after the first two. Achieving success in each year would give momentum to the following year.

Jalen agreed to continue the goals and review them with John each semester. Jalen knew he was lucky to have such a great resource; John was grateful to give back to the next generation.

THE FOUR CHOICES:

BILLY – University, out-of-state tuition & live on campus
SHANICE – Community college and live at home
SOFIA – University, live on campus
JALEN – Community college, work, live at home

The Costs of Each Student's Choice

Decision Costs	Billy	Shanice	Sofia	Jalen
Tuition Year 1	$ 38,484	$ 4,810	$ 17,244	$ 4,810
Tuition Year 2	38,484	4,810	17,244	4,810
Tuition Year 3	38,484	17,244	17,244	17,244
Tuition Year 4	38,484	17,244	17,244	17,244
Room and Board Year 1	14,400	-	14,400	-
Room and Board Year 2	14,400	-	14,400	-
Room and Board Year 3	14,400	-	14,400	-
Room and Board Year 4	14,400	-	14,400	-
Total Costs of Degree	211,536	44,108	126,576	44,108
Expense Reductions				
Tuition Reimbursement Year 1				(4,810)
Tuition Reimbursement Year 2				(4,810)
Tuition Reimbursement Year 3				(5,250)
Tuition Reimbursement Year 4				(5,250)
Take-home Wages while working Year 1				(13,000)
Wages while working Year 2				(13,000)
Wages while working Year 3				(13,000)
Wages while working Year 4				(13,000)
Total Reduction of Expenses:				(72,120)
Total Debt	$ 211,536	$ 44,108	$ 126,576	$ (28,012)

Billy, Sofia, Shanice, and Jalen all end up meeting at CU in their final two years of college. They don't discuss their decisions and financial impacts with each other while still in school. As they all get closer to graduation, they all interview with local engineering firms. To illustrate the financial impact of their education decisions, we need to give them an identical future, so we will say they are all hired at IBM, which has a large engineering campus just outside of Boulder, Colorado.

They all start with the same salary, and they all move up the ranks of IBM together, each receiving the same salary increases and job promotions. They also all have similar life expenses after college, with one striking difference: the amount each will pay in student loans each month.

While our worksheet shows that Jalen could have graduated from college with money from his job earnings, we will assume for our future that Jalen spent all of these earnings on other expenses he might have had along realize.

Consider that we only included tuition plus room and board for all of our examples, but we know that life has other expenses. What about a car, gas, insurance? Want to go out and have some fun, that's all extra expenses and there can be many of them along the way, like laundry. Assuming there were some side jobs or family help for those expenses, we can focus on just the impact of the costs of tuition and room and board.

A Look at the Income and Life Expenses after College Before Student Loan Payments:

Income and Expenses Years 1-5			
Income:			62,000.00
FICA Taxes:		7.65%	(4,743.00)
Income Taxes:		22.00%	(13,640.00)
Income after taxes			43,617.00
401K plan		3%	(1,860.00)
Monthly Living Expenses:			(27,960.00)
Student Loan Payment			-
Disposable Income Available			13,797.00
Monthly Expenses:			
	Rent		900.00
	Utilities		150.00
	Car & Gas		400.00
	Car Insurance		100.00
	Cell Phone		80.00
	Food		400.00
	Entertainment		200.00
	Clothing		100.00
	Total Montly Bills		2,330.00

What College Choices Mean for Life After College

Assuming, as described above, that Billy, Sofia, Shanice, and Jalen all have the same expenses after school, their financial lives will be significantly different. The amount each will be required to pay back in student loans, based on their choices, is very different.

Based on a repayment period of 20 years at 7% interest, here are each of their loan payments:

- Billy's loan payment each month will be $1,640
- Shanice's loan payment each month will be $342
- Sofia's loan payment each month will be $981
- And Jalen has no payment because he paid all his expenses along the way.

Updates on Prices:

All of these prices were done in 2020 and 2021, before inflation really started. I've left the original prices so students and parents can update these worksheets on their own and understand how inflation may impact your financial future. Expenses have gone up more than incomes. Perhaps your income will be higher, but perhaps your expenses will rise even more as well.

On the other side of inflation are interest rates, also rising. That makes the cost of debt more expensive, increasing the size of the loan payment to repay debt.

This is a horrible one-two punch for students, higher costs for school, and higher cost of debt.

A Look at Billy's Income and Expenses After College:

Income and Expenses Years 1-5			
Income:			62,000.00
FICA Taxes:		7.65%	(4,743.00)
Income Taxes:		22.00%	(13,640.00)
Income after taxes			43,617.00
401K plan		3%	(1,860.00)
Monthly Living Expenses:			(27,960.00)
Student Loan Payment			(19,680.44)
Disposable Income Available			(5,883.44)
Monthly Expenses:			
	Rent		900.00
	Utilities		150.00
	Car & Gas		400.00
	Car Insurance		100.00
	Cell Phone		80.00
	Food		400.00
	Entertainment		200.00
	Clothing		100.00
	Total Monthly Bills		2,330.00

Billy will not earn enough to pay for his living expenses and his school loan payments after he pays taxes and his monthly living expenses. He will use credit cards to live the same lifestyle as his peers and will fall deeper into debt each year, despite raises and promotions.

A Look at Sofia's Income and Expenses After College:

Income and Expenses Years 1-5			
Income:			62,000.00
FICA Taxes:		7.65%	(4,743.00)
Income Taxes:		22.00%	(13,640.00)
Income after taxes			43,617.00
401K plan		3%	(1,860.00)
Monthly Living Expenses:			(27,960.00)
Student Loan Payment			(11,776.11)
Disposable Income Available			2,020.89
Monthly Expenses:			
	Rent		900.00
	Utilities		150.00
	Car & Gas		400.00
	Car Insurance		100.00
	Cell Phone		80.00
	Food		400.00
	Entertainment		200.00
	Clothing		100.00
	Total Montly Bills		2,330.00

Sofia will have a tough five years as she will barely make enough to pay her expenses. Once she receives promotions and raises, she will have enough disposable income to have some fun. She will wish she could have saved more for retirement sooner and will wait to start a family until her debt is lower, even though she is ready a few years out of school.

A Look at Shanice's Income and Expenses After College:

Shanice will have disposable income every month since her payments are very manageable. Life will be good.

Income and Expenses Years 1-5			
Income:			62,000.00
FICA Taxes:		7.65%	(4,743.00)
Income Taxes:		22.00%	(13,640.00)
Income after taxes			43,617.00
401K plan		3%	(1,860.00)
Monthly Living Expenses:			(27,960.00)
Student Loan Payment			(4,103.63)
Disposable Income Available			9,693.37
Monthly Expenses:			
	Rent		900.00
	Utilities		150.00
	Car & Gas		400.00
	Car Insurance		100.00
	Cell Phone		80.00
	Food		400.00
	Entertainment		200.00
	Clothing		100.00
	Total Montly Bills		2,330.00

A Look at Jalen's Income & Expenses After College:

Jalen will have the best time of all of them in his 20's and 30's as his efforts to work and pay for school means he can take all of that money others are paying for loans and spend it on experiences and a better life for his family.

Income and Expenses Years 1-5			
Income:			62,000.00
FICA Taxes:		7.65%	(4,743.00)
Income Taxes:		22.00%	(13,640.00)
Income after taxes			43,617.00
401K plan		3%	(1,860.00)
Monthly Living Expenses:			(27,960.00)
Student Loan Payment			-
Disposable Income Available			13,797.00
Monthly Expenses:			
	Rent		900.00
	Utilities		150.00
	Car & Gas		400.00
	Car Insurance		100.00
	Cell Phone		80.00
	Food		400.00
	Entertainment		200.00
	Clothing		100.00
	Total Montly Bills		2,330.00

As each of our Heroes move up at IBM, their Incomes increase. To make all of these situations comparable, we will assume they all move up at the same rate and their annual earnings rise every 5 years, but to make things look better, we won't increase the expenses for any of them. Before student loan payments their earnings in future years look like this:

Income and Expenses		Years 5-10	Years 11-15	Years 16-20
Income:		72,000.00	85,000.00	95,000.00
FICA Taxes:	7.65%	(5,508.00)	(6,502.50)	(7,267.50)
Income Taxes:	24.00%	(17,280.00)	(20,400.00)	(22,800.00)
Income after taxes		49,212.00	58,097.50	64,932.50
401K plan	3%	(2,160.00)	(2,550.00)	(2,850.00)
Monthly Living Expenses:		(27,960.00)	(27,960.00)	(27,960.00)
Student Loan Payment		-	-	-
Disposable Income Available		19,092.00	27,587.50	34,122.50
Monthly Expenses:				
Rent		900.00	900.00	900.00
Utilities		150.00	150.00	150.00
Car & Gas		400.00	400.00	400.00
Car Insurance		100.00	100.00	100.00
Cell Phone		80.00	80.00	80.00
Food		400.00	400.00	400.00
Entertainment		200.00	200.00	200.00
Clothing		100.00	100.00	100.00
Total Monthly Bills		2,330.00	2,330.00	2,330.00

Now let's take a look at all of their financial lives twenty years later. We can keep everything else the same for each of them and examine only the choices of debt and the impact of that debt in the future. Assuming every five years everyone got a raise and promotion, and all of their living expenses were the same, we can easily examine the debt by itself. Let's also assume they all contributed equally to their retirement accounts and invested their remaining disposable income. We have low rates of return, to not exaggerate the differences, so all their retirement accounts and savings accounts pay 5%, and credit card debt costs 15%.

While we know that they would make different choices and have varying expenses, this example allows us to examine the situation with all other things being equal. Twenty years after graduation from college, receiving promotions and all making almost $100,000 per year, they are all in very different financial situations.

After 20 Years:	Billy	Shanice	Sofia	Jalen
Retirement plan	128,741	128,741	128,741	128,741
Savings	-	320,521	66,823	456,211
CC Debt	(150,178)	-	-	-
Total Net Worth	(21,437)	449,261	195,564	584,952

After 20 years, Billy has finally paid off his student loan debts, but because his payments were so large and he had to live on credit cards, he owes over $150,000 of credit card debt. He has never been able to save enough to open his own engineering firm as he had dreamed.

Shanice has done well. Her low student loan monthly payment has allowed her to save, and after twenty years, she has accumulated almost $450,000.

Sofia has done pretty good. While she would like to have saved more, her high student loan payment means that after twenty years, she has about $195,000 saved.

Jalen has seen the most rewards for his efforts. While the four years of college were very hard on him, that work experience was invaluable and has given him a lot of options. He has saved almost $585,000.

Takeaways from Choices

- We like to say that there are no right or wrong choices, but is that true? The choices we make will impact the amount we pay and the amount of debt we carry into the future. For some students, that debt will destroy their future. It is not a crisis if there are no problems and it is beyond a crisis!
- The amount of debt you leave school with will have a direct impact on your ability to live the life you want moving forward. It is hard to see the impact of your decisions when you are young, but the effect of debt can last a lifetime. What if you had similar debts to Billy but a job that didn't pay as much? As bad as Billy's debt is today, it could be a lot worse.
- These discussions do not show the additional problem of inflation. Due to profligate government deficits, we will be living with inflation for years to come, perhaps decades. That will increase the cost of living, making debt repayment even more difficult as your daily expenses increase.

PART 9

The Total Cost of Debt

The total cost of debt is impossible to calculate. As discussed earlier, does debt increase your stress? If so, how do we measure the cost of your added stress? Will student loan debt lower your credit score? With a lower credit score, will that cause you to pay higher interest rates on other borrowing such as credit cards, a home or car loan? How much higher will the rates that you have to pay be? Will a lower credit score prevent you from buying a home or making other investments that could increase your wealth? A 1% increase in interest rate could mean you pay 13% more for a home! Rates matter, so does your credit score and starting from behind is dangerous.

One thing is certain: Paying off debt will certainly keep you from saving. Saving creates opportunities. From a bigger picture for society, more debt will mean fewer opportunities for everyone. In our "**Four Lives, Four Choices**" example, Billy wanted to start an engineering firm and perhaps could have developed products that would make all our lives better. But that dream of Billy's will never happen because he is saddled with debt. How can you afford to take a few years of trial and error, meanwhile making nothing as an entrepreneur, when you are in debt? You can't, and society is worse off because of it.

When you carry large amounts of debt, it harms your credit score. This can mean that all of the other expenses in life where you need financing, like buying a car or a house, will cost you

Total debt cost is hard to calculate, but should include the following:

» Stress impact
» Credit score impact
» Higher interest rates on loans
» Inability to save money
» Inability to have life experiences

more for financing than if you didn't have the student loan debt. How much more is hard to say, but having poor credit can easily make everything 20% more expensive, which means you have even fewer opportunities going forward because you have a higher cost of money.

How can you afford to save for a down payment on a house when you already have sizable loans to repay? Likely you cannot, so you will have to forego buying assets and investing in a home or other assets that could make you money. It is hard to take a chance to work for a startup that can't pay you as much but offers stock incentives when you have loans to repay.

Most importantly, what will be the impact of the debt on your ability to live the life you want, and what will be the impact of that on you emotionally? How could we possibly measure the value of missed experiences and feeling forced to work in a job that is not fulfilling?

Debt's Impact on Your Psyche

Jalen had worked so hard to get his degree without any debt. He graduated with a few thousand dollars in his bank account after paying for all his college expenses, including his car, which, although older, would have to wait to be replaced. He decided to live at home for two more years after college and stay in his same childhood room, but give the money he would otherwise pay for rent to his mother. Jalen knew she had helped him tremendously, just by providing support and paying the rent while he went to school. When Jalen sat down with John and reviewed all of the costs, he couldn't help but see the $15,000 per year that his mother was contributing. Jalen wanted to repay this debt to his mother, but he wanted it to go to her retirement account.

After two years of giving back, continuing to live with his mother, Jalen was excited to move out. He spoke to John about this decision, and John advised him on the amount he should spend on rent and suggested he find a roommate. After finding a roommate Jalen felt he could live with, and moving out on his own, Jalen was ready for his reward. He was smart enough not to buy a new car, but he knew what he wanted, a full size, four-wheel-drive SUV that he could take to the mountains in the summer and winter. He was ready to enjoy Colorado!

The first day Jalen pulled into the work parking lot in the Jeep Grand Cherokee, Billy was pulling in at the same time. Jalen and Billy had been working together on a couple of projects and over beers after work one day Billy had confided in Jalen and told him how big his student loan payment was, over $1,500 per month. That was more than Jalen was paying for rent and his recently acquired, lightly used Jeep. Billy was obviously a bit jealous based on his remark to Jalen that he "didn't need the Jeep", but Jalen knew that comment was coming from Billy's frustration with his decisions on his college debt and the hole he had dug for himself.

That night, Jalen stopped by John's place to catch up and show him the new Jeep. John was proud of Jalen, knew that he had worked so hard, and he deserved his reward of a new vehicle. Jalen was thinking about Billy and his next twenty years of a $1,500/month student loan payment. Jalen expressed his gratitude to John for helping him make the decisions that were now allowing him to reap the benefits of his efforts.

Jalen remembered wanting to go straight to CU and just borrow all the money, thinking that his community college experience would somehow be less worthwhile. He knew that without John's advice and discussions with him, he probably would have made that choice. If that had happened, he too would be saddled with tons of debt, just like Billy. As tears streamed down his face, Jalen thanked John for taking the time to show him the cost of debt and talking with him about where learning really happens. What John had done for him was life changing, and he promised to pay it forward.

John was overwhelmed by Jalen's emotions that night as Jalen cried on his shoulder. Jalen told John about Billy's situation, and he could feel how much that debt was going to be a problem for Billy for decades to come. Why was he so lucky to have a John in his life when Billy didn't? Or maybe Billy just didn't listen, Jalen didn't know, but he could now see the consequences of the prior decision in front of him, and it made him very sad for Billy.

John felt as though his part in Jalen's journey had been simple and easy and knew that it was Jalen who did the work; he was just a friendly neighbor. Jalen agreed, but asked John, "What if you hadn't been that guide for me? I'd be stuck, giving up most of what I worked so hard for to someone else. I wouldn't be showing you my new car; I'd be paying for someone else's."

The Jeep is just one example of the many ways in which Jalen's life will differ from Billy's in the coming decades. Jalen will have the financial freedom to pursue whatever business opportunities he encounters instead of being concerned about paying debts. He will be able to spend his earnings on life experiences and travel and will not have the stress of those monthly student loan payments hanging over him. He can choose who he works for and the type of work he pursues. He has control over his life's decisions because he lacks the debt burden that Billy took on. He will be able to save money each month, and that savings will create more opportunities.

While it does not seem to be part of the initial conversation about student loan debt, in many respects this is an important question: What future opportunities will student loan debt prevent you from having?

Debt's Hidden Burden – Job Choice

While we can measure the financial costs that student loans will bring, what about the effect it will have on the job you want to pursue? As we discussed in Chapter 4, while most students who get into Ivy League schools do not express an interest in the

Elite Professional Service (EPS) firms before they begin college, a staggering 70% of Harvard seniors apply for jobs at the EPS firms. Why so many? It's not because they believe it will be rewarding work. Harvard graduates can certainly do the math, and if they are able to secure one of these high-paying jobs it can be a substantial help in paying down their student loan debts. This is especially true for MBA and JD (law) programs.

But as we have seen, high debts are not just for those at the Ivy Plus schools, as state school tuition plus room and board typically exceeds $100,000 per year. What about all of those students? Many will end up in jobs that they do not enjoy because they have the burden of student loan debt. Many students would prefer working in something they have a passion for, such as a non-profit organization that helps the homeless or social work jobs that help those with disabilities. These jobs usually do not pay as well but can be more personally fulfilling than an office job or an EPS firm.

Student loans can prevent you from having the job you want, where you feel required to work in a job that you hate because it pays enough to pay off your loans. While much of the focus of this book is on the lifetime increase of earnings, money is certainly not the key to happiness. Without enough to pay our bills, life is certainly miserable, but studies show that the law of dimensioning returns also applies to our earnings. While some people will use money as a status and power symbol and no amount is enough, most of us, when we begin to make about $75,000 per year (in 2020 dollars) find that more money is not worth the additional effort and does not change much in our lifestyle.

But if you have large debts to pay off, working at a job you love may not be an option for you as you have to work at a job you need because of all of your debts. This is a very hidden burden that is not discussed enough, but I have heard about over and over from so many people stuck in jobs they do not enjoy. There are so many Billys out there who never get to start their own firms.

As an entrepreneur myself, this topic is close to my heart. So many 'would be entrepreneurs' are stuck in jobs they do not like and would love to start their own business, but student loan debt is preventing them from saving enough to pursue those dreams. This makes me very sad, and if you want to start your own business, please take heed, debt, especially student loan debt will make this harder for you.

For everyone, less debt makes life's future choices easier, where you have the opportunities to take a job you like versus being forced to work in a job you don't. Put a price on that!

The Real Cost of Debt

If you buy stock in Apple, what have you purchased? You've purchased the right to the future earnings of the company (usually given in the form of a dividend), a vote on who should run the company, and a right to sell that share if you disagree with management's decisions.

When someone loans you money, what are they buying from you? A right to your future earnings. When it comes to student loan debt, that future right, of the person loaning the money, is as close to a guarantee as it gets, and they can enforce that right to make you pay. Because of the laws surrounding student loans, you will have to pay them, whether they have to garnish your wages all the way to your Social Security checks, or you pay them off early. When you take out debt, you give up a right to your future earnings and what you could otherwise do with those earnings.

When you give up your right to your future earnings, you are giving up your ability to live the life you want to live. Instead of paying off debt, you could take your earnings and invest them to make you money so you can reach financial independence and are not forced to work for anyone you don't want to. You could take your earnings and buy yourself experiences, a home, or take yourself out to dinner. You can go to concerts, take trips to visit family and friends, or help your family with unexpected expenses. If you can accumulate and save, you can become financially independent, where you no longer have to work or are financially secure enough that you can work in a job that you enjoy, even though it pays you less money or even no money at all. You can start a business and work for yourself.

The real cost of debt is your freedom. There are many things that people say they would like to have but cannot because of their debt burdens. These extend beyond the material items, such as buying a home into family decisions about having children or having more children. When you are burdened by debt, you lose so many of the freedoms that directly link to happiness, including:

- Your freedom to choose where you want to work or to work at all.
- Your freedom to choose with whom you want to work.
- Your freedom to spend what you earn because when you're in debt, your money doesn't belong to you.
- The freedom to not have to think about whom you owe and live with the stress of that burden.
- The freedom to live where you want to live, not where you have to live so you can repay debts and still afford rent.

- The freedom to have experiences or take your family on experiences together.
- The freedom to help others.

All debts can take away these freedoms, but almost all other debts (except not paying your taxes), you can get removed if they become too burdensome through the bankruptcy process. Student loan debt stays for life, and the cost of your freedom will last as long as the debt does. The lost opportunities may be lost forever.

The Value of Family Help

The decision to pursue a university degree is typically a family decision. Parents and communities want their children to do better in life and have more opportunities than they were given, especially when young people have the aptitude to excel in their educational pursuits. The most, let me repeat that, the MOST critical part of family support is emotional.

Much of the value of a degree from an employer's perspective is the length of time it takes to get a degree. It shows that you can stick with a task and achieve the goal despite the obstacles placed in your path. Four years or more is a long time, and a large percentage of people, as shown in the statistics, don't make it through to receive a diploma. Having family support is crucial to all education, and college is no different. We all need emotional support to keep us going when times get tough. Family helps us to stay the course and complete the degree, so you don't end up in the worst situation: in debt with no degree.

Before we go any further, let me clarify. Help from the family does not mean that the family agrees with the student on all matters. Adults need to act like adults. You would not support your child buying a new car that they cannot afford, and you should not help them with tens of thousands of dollars in loans when there are alternative solutions. As the parent/adult, you cannot accept the idea that a college education is "priceless." It is not priceless; it specifically has a price, usually too high to justify. Let's not forget that the student is chasing a dream where money seems inconsequential and they lack the personal experience to understand the consequences of their decisions, especially around debt. Hence, we have a crisis! Not enough parents are learning about the business of education and preventing their children from making a poor choice about how much debt and in many cases, taking on too much debt themselves for their children.

> **The most critical family support is emotional.**
>
> **You will never receive a *priceless* education from a school.**

Family support needs to begin at the student's decision to go to college, and includes all the financial considerations, geographic considerations, and what the family can offer in support. Many parents are willing to take on massive amounts of debt because they see that as the only path forward for their child. But there are a lot of paths and choosing one that does not hurt the family financially is very important as well.

As the data show, the cost of college can be separated into two parts: tuition, and room and board. We have discussed that one way to reduce tuition is to attend a community college for the first two years. If, as a parent, all you can help with is putting a roof over your child's head and helping them with food, you are still providing HALF of the cost. Don't discount that as it is a huge value. While not the ideal situation for either party, it is usually the best financial decision for the family.

Most children may also need to understand that they, themselves, are not easy to live with either. Parents are usually ready for their kids to move out, but in today's world that means giving up too much of your future earnings if you're going to pay to live on a college campus for four years. If it is at all possible to live at home, do it! It will be much better than moving back home after college because you have so much debt you cannot afford your own place.

Takeaways on the Real Cost of Debt

» Calculating the total impact of debt is very hard. If we include stress and the impact on your ability to lead the life you want to after college, what is that cost?

» When you graduate from college it will feel like a great accomplishment, but if you have a lot of debt, then the real challenge has just begun. How are you going to feel when you have to move back home, cannot afford the car you want or the trip you want to take?

» Would you rather feel like Jalen, grateful to not have the burden of student loan debt and excited about the opportunities you have in front of you?

» You cannot know the negative impact on your psyche of debt until it too late.

» Most of us want to go to college so we can pursue an area of interest that we want to work in. But many of us do not think about whether we will be able to take the job we want because we have too much debt. No one want to feel forced into a job that pays more, that they like less, because of debt burdens.

» Freedom comes from not being restricted. When you take out student debt, you give up the right to your future income and therefore your future freedoms to pursue what you want. This can prevent you from opening a business, buying a home, starting a family, or living where you want to live.

PART 10

Building Your Plan

You have answered all of the questions regarding your college plan to get your degree. You know why you are pursuing a degree. You have learned about yourself and the system of higher education. You have a budget and have figured out the family help that you can expect. You have set a goal of how much debt you will take on (hopefully minimal), and you have learned how to hack the system. You have examined the examples, and you understand that debt is a right to your future earnings, and you want to keep those for yourself as much as possible.

Now you need to put it all together into your college plan.

The Goal:

Why do you believe a college education is right for you?

____

____

____

____

What do you hope the degree you are seeking will bring you and your family?

____

____

____

____

If you know what job you want after you graduate, what is it? What degree do you need to obtain this job? If you don't know, who has a job or career that seems interesting to you that you might like to do?

____

____

____

____

What does the job pay – starting salary through 10 years of experience?

Year 1 _______________

Year 5 _______________

Year 10 _______________

How much of the additional value of what you will earn are you willing to give up getting your degree? (Our old friend, Mary, is giving up about 40% of all her additional earnings) Assuming the additional value is $550k of earnings, how much of that are you willing to give up getting that degree?

____________%

Building Your Plan:

Which University do you want to get a degree from?

____

Which community college will you attend for the first two years?

____

What will be your total expenses?

Year 1: Tuition ________________

Room & Board: ______________

Year 2: Tuition ________________

Room & Board: ______________

Year 3: Tuition ________________

Room & Board: ______________

Year 4: Tuition ________________

Room & Board: ______________

Total for all: _____________________________

If you plan on working, which employer have you chosen who has tuition reimbursement: ________________

Second Option: ____________________

Third Option: ____________________

Where will the money come from?

Family money available: ________________

Scholarships: ________________

Federal Aid: ________________

Job Earnings: ________________

Job Tuition Reimbursement: ________________

If you are going to take on any debt, what is your maximum amount?

____

What will that monthly payment be and for how long?

Amount: $___________

Years to Repay all Debt: _________

Everyone in the Family Do Their Part

The planning for college should be part of a family decision. Parents and students should go through this process together. If the family were going to spend $120,000 on anything else, how long would that decision take? How much information would you gather? How much scrutiny would there be over the decision?

Most families will never spend $120,000 on a single experience. Many people don't spend that much money when buying a home. The home may cost more, but the down payment is usually much less than $120k. Everyone involved in this process should understand the system of higher education, know the costs involved and spend the appropriate amount of time to make an informed decision.

Hopefully, this guide is helping you figure out the right questions to ask before embarking on the so-called "tried and true" college journey. It is up to you to devise the best plan for you and your family. I recommend a goal of zero debt, but I also understand why that can be difficult to achieve. I recommend a job while in school, but I understand why some people may not want to work

As an employer, if I were interviewing two candidates who were equally qualified, and one had taken out loans to go through college, had a lot of debt and no work experience; while the other had worked and had no debt, there is no question who I would hire. The experiences of working while going to school offer life lessons in many areas, and these experiences can be equally as important and valuable as what you learn in a classroom. Remember, life is an educational journey; it does not end after college. If you are going to be a professional, the real learning begins after university.

Parents, you have the experience in life to know the burden of debt. Share your experiences and do your best to guide your children into a debt-free future. Do not take on debt burdens yourself to try to give your children a better life, it is not required, and your child is not old enough to fully understand how those burdens will affect you both into the future. Do not accept that debt is the only way forward and be the leader of your family to protect your family's future earnings.

Students: Have a plan: set goals, short-term and long-term. Just because you cannot find an employer this year with tuition reimbursement does not mean they will not be hiring next year. If you really want to work at UPS, figure out a way to do it. Continue to ask for an opportunity and refuse to accept "no" as an answer. Any "no" towards what you want should be taken as just a "no" today; any good salesperson will tell you that.

Obstacles will be put in your path to see if you want to achieve your goals. Know that we all face these obstacles, and the difficult parts you push through create the sweetness when a dream is realized. The view from the top of a mountain might not look as spectacular to someone who just drove up the road, but it is spectacular to those who climbed from the bottom because of the effort required. Embrace the difficulty; it is what makes the accomplishment great!

Get a Head Start

If you know that a college degree is your path, then there are many ways you can get a head start. Many college-bound students will take Advanced Placement courses, hoping they will pass the AP test and that the school they are enrolling in will accept those tests for college course credit. But why risk those credits on a test? What if you have a bad day on test day? Why not take the courses at a local community college instead?

Most high schools now have opportunities for students to take college courses at the local community college. If you take courses that transfer to state schools, as most are required to, then by taking the community college courses, you guarantee that those credits are going to transfer, so long as you pass the class. This is better than the AP course where the test matters, and it is no guarantee that the AP test will result in college credits.

Pathway programs like (this) the Career and Technical Education program for Colorado students can help all students, whether seeking a technical career or a 4-year degree.

The best part: most of the classes will be free while you are still in high school.

PART 11

Strategies for Your Family Situation

Strategy is the art of figuring out what to do based on the situation. Your situation is different than others, but many of us share similar obstacles. As an athlete in college, I met a lot of different people from different backgrounds, and we all discussed our lives back home and what type of family support we received. Some students had no family support, some had a lot, and many were in the middle, including myself. I had an old, two-wheel drive, two-seater truck in college, and many of my teammates considered me rich just because I had a car. It was only through meeting people in tougher situations than my own did I become grateful for the support I had instead of believing my family should have provided me with more support.

In this chapter, we will explore strategies for prospective students from different family situations, all aimed at the same goal of graduating from college with no student loan debt.

No Family Support, Can't (Or Won't) Live at Home

It is a truly difficult situation for anyone, at any part of life, to not have emotional family support. Almost always, this is no fault of the student (unless you can't figure out how to stop getting arrested). Unfortunately, many people project their insecurities onto their children, and especially stepchildren. Emotional support is often more critical than financial support. Our community can give us strength and increase our willpower muscle just by believing in us and helping us stay the course when we feel exhausted or hopeless. Hopefully, even if you have no economic support, you can at least get your parents to fill out the Federal Student Aid form so you can get government grants for school. You should also be eligible for state grants to pay for tuition.

If it is an option, try to live with a friend who is going to school. This could mean living with your friend and their parents or finding someone who is on the same path as you and being roommates. This situation could not only help with lower expenses but also give you a support structure.

If this is not available, consider a smaller school in a town that has a lower cost of living. While my college choices were influenced heavily by the opportunity to play basketball, one of the reasons I chose the community college I attended was because there was a low cost of living. In all honesty, it was not the greatest town, but it got me where I wanted to go at a low cost, so the sacrifice of the traditional "college experience" was worth the future opportunities that came from having no student loan debts.

Start at a community college unless you can receive need- and merit-based scholarships to cover all (or close to all) of the tuition and room and board expenses of a university. Sometimes, at smaller state schools where tuition and room and board are less expensive, grants and work-study can cover all of the costs. But for most of us, community college is still the right place to start.

Typically, governor's grants can help pay tuition for community college, and if you are eligible for a Federal Pell Grant, that is another $6,000 to help with your living expenses. If this is your situation, you may consider not working your first year to give yourself space and time to adjust to life on your own. But, be frugal. Any amount of your Pell Grant that you can save, along with any wages you can earn from a job, can help you pay your future tuition once you transfer to a university.

If you are eligible for a Governor's Grant, then the employer tuition reimbursement is not as important to you, and often you will also qualify for a work-study job on campus. I had both a Governor's Grant and work-study during my second year of college. The Governor's Grant paid for tuition and books, and the work-study job helped pay for rent and food. I wasn't eligible for a Federal Pell grant, but most of my friends who were did not spend their money wisely. If you are on your own, hopefully you will have the foresight to save for future tuition.

The most important thing you can do to keep your expenses down is to find low-cost rent. But you still want to put yourself in a situation that supports your education, so a room in a house where everyone is 18- or 19-years old and partying all the time may not be the best transition for you. I saw a lot of decent students become poor students because of their living situation. If you want to go to the big state school when you transfer, then keeping your costs down and saving while in community college is key to being able to afford the higher tuition for those final two years. I rented a room off-campus for my two years of junior college and paid $200/month rent. It wasn't anything fancy, but in college, fancy is not a need.

Choosing a smaller town to go to community college may not be ideal, but remember, it's a sacrifice for a better future, and your future self is congratulating you on a wise choice. The transition to a larger school will be significant, especially finding new roommates and a job with tuition reimbursement to help supplement the tuition cost. If you work, get tuition reimbursement from an employer, and get a Federal Pell Grant, that should cover all of your expenses so you can graduate with no debt.

If you need to leave home, have no family support, and are not eligible for a Federal Pell Grant, then you will need to find an employer with tuition reimbursement. The rest of the path remains the same, but if you want to graduate from the big state school, it may require some student loan debt. This is a challenging path for anyone, and it may be wise to choose military service to help with the transition and then be supported by the GI Bill, or move to Louisville and work for UPS as they will pay for all of school. Also, remember Starbucks will pay for all tuition for Arizona State online.

Family Support For Living, But Not Tuition

Now that you have learned that half of the cost of college is for room and board, you realize that just being able to provide room and board is massive support for any student. It might not be ideal to keep living at home, but isn't it better to live at home at 18, than move back home at 22 with a ton of debt to pay off?

Living at home and attending the first two years at community college is the easiest way for most students to reduce their overall college bill and related debt. If your family cannot help pay your tuition but has a high enough household income that you are not eligible for a Federal Pell Grant, then work-study or a part-time job should be enough to cover the tuition costs at community college.

Finding an employer with tuition reimbursement that can cover the cost of tuition means all the income you earn you get to keep, and it can pay for all the other living expenses you may have, or you can save it to help pay down your tuition for the final two years at a 4-year university.

If you are eligible for a Federal Pell Grant, then it's likely you will also be able to receive a Governor's Grant. Sometimes, you are eligible for the state governor's grants if you have tuition costs paid through an employer, and almost always, you'll be awarded the Federal Pell Grant if your tuition is covered through other grants. The idea is that this money will help with room and board instead of tuition. Hopefully, you see the hacks here.

If you have a job that helps pay your community college tuition, you could potentially receive the Governor's and Federal Pell Grants in the form of a check to you. You can save these amounts for your final two years of tuition. Or, if your Governor's grant covers your community college tuition and books, then you can decide not to work and still save the Federal Pell Grant money for future tuition costs. Living at home just gave you a lot of options to save money to cover those costs!

Jalen's story showed us the path to no debt while having a job and living at home. His is the blueprint for anyone who can live at home and wants to graduate with no debt.

Even with no family support for tuition and no eligibility for Federal or State Grants, it is possible to graduate with no debt. Here, the key is finding an employer like UPS to receive tuition reimbursement.

Family Support for Living and Tuition

The college choice decision for families who can afford to send their children off to school and pay the cost of tuition and room and board are interesting to me. I hesitate to call it wasteful because most parents want to give their children the "college experience" and don't want them to have to worry about the money. However, the families who can afford to pay for it all are not as numerous as they would have you believe. If we used the car example, none of these families would want their child to be the one who pays a lot more for the car that could have been purchased for less. But college is a strange choice, wrapped in emotions and a desire for a "coming of age" experience to jumpstart the transition into adulthood.

Hopefully, students in the lucky position to have their family's help realize that they are very fortunate to have the financial support. While I knew that my family's financial support would be minimal, I appreciate all that I did receive because I was friends with many people who had no help at all. Just having the car insurance paid seemed like a big deal. But even if you have the money, wouldn't you rather spend it frugally, so there is some left to help you transition into adulthood?

Many families are in a position where there is some savings for college expenses, alongside a high willingness to pay for the additional costs by taking out loans. It's what we all have been sold as the thing to do, and it is middle-class families who typically take on too much debt in all forms, as they try to keep up with the wealthier families who can truly afford it. "Jonesing" is a societal problem, and an easy trap for parents to fall into, especially when children have their hearts set on getting accepted to a highly ranked school. Parents don't want to dampen that desire for achievement or have their child feeling that they fall short when compared to their peers.

Many students end up like Sofia, with large amounts of debt despite some financial support. The decision not to live at home and to pay high tuition at the university for four years can add up to a lot of unnecessary debt.

Hopefully, going through this course has changed your opinion on the value proposition of college, and you now understand the value of living at home during college. Or, in the situation where your family has the money, if you can graduate and have the money for room and board to start your life, that will be a huge plus and create a lot of opportunities like house hacking being done by Matt, whose roommates are paying his mortgage.

If you have family support, be grateful for it and take advantage of it. Live at home to make that money last longer. Parents, if you have that money to spend, set it aside for after graduation. If your family can afford partial tuition support, then use the money available wisely. Consider a job that can also contribute to tuition reimbursement, and if you are not eligible for federal or state grants, put more effort into finding other scholarships that you may qualify for or a job with tuition reimbursement. Pick a school that works with what you want to do instead of just the largest state school that has the highest tuition. Community college credits still count the same, so don't get sold on the four years at university with high tuition and room and board costs.

Often, when we have the money available, or the ability to borrow, it makes us complacent. We don't think about the situation enough because we *can afford it.* But just because you can afford to pay more for that same Honda Accord doesn't mean you should. The family should spend a lot of time discussing the decisions and the opportunities that may not be available in the future based on the current choices. As we explored in Chapter 6, family money is still finite and would often better be used to jump-start adult life versus no money or worse, lots of debt, that will do the opposite.

> ***The life lessons for someone who figures out how to pay for it all on their own may be more useful than the college degree itself.***

Family Situation, Final Thoughts

Each of our family situations is slightly different, but depending on our circumstances, we have various opportunities to take advantage of, and we will get different learning experiences. While it is great when a family can afford to pay for everything, ***the life lessons for someone who figures***

out how to pay for it all on their own may be more useful than the college degree itself.

Take advantage of whatever support that is available to you and be grateful for it. If you are eligible for federal and state grants, be wise with them and save them during community college years for the final two years. Getting the degree you want without debt is possible if you use the support available to you wisely.

If you have no support at all, you can still get the degree you want without debt, but if you really want it from the big state school, you might have to choose military service first, but that may prove to be a good thing to help you transition into adulthood.

I know, and have met, a lot of people who have college degrees. I don't know anyone who wishes they had more college debt and I know a lot of people who wish they had less. It is hard to understand the debt experience unless it happens to you but I'm hopeful this book has helped you understand the burden that debt can be on the rest of your life and how it can hold you back from fulfilling your dreams.

We need more decisions like Jalen's and fewer Billy's.

END OF BOOK NOTES

You did it! You've finished the book and hopefully you've learned a lot—about yourself, your family situation, and the various ways to get what you want without sacrificing your future.

Now it's up to you to choose wisely. Remember you won't always be young, that life is long, the lessons are plentiful and student loan debt is ***Special Debt***. The mistake of this debt could one of the harder lessons in life that could follow you around for decades to come. Imagine your future self…. when you're 40 and still paying $1,000+ a month on your student loans, do you think you'll still consider your college experience *worth it* or *priceless*, after you've sacrificed the nicer car, the vacations, the house, or even having children? Perhaps, but unlikely. Hopefully this book has helped you think about better ways to get to where you want to be, without sacrificing for decades to come. Please, don't destroy your future with debt!

SUPPLEMENT 1

Condensed History of Student Loan Crisis

If you are interested in how student loans came to be so out of control, then this section is for you. It is not relevant to making better decisions today to keep yourself out of debt, but it is an interesting story of fear, bad laws, unintended consequences, and the lack of the government to make meaningful changes when laws cause citizens significant harm.

So how did we arrive at a place where a sociology major has $200,000 of student loan debt? How is it even possible?

As I outlined in the Keep Yours "The Real Math" podcast, the amount of earnings required to repay the loans is two- to three- times the amount borrowed, depending on the interest rate and loan duration. But this math only tells half the story. What about when Billy wants or needs a credit card? A car loan? To buy a house? None of these are going to be easy at any time in the near future for Billy. Nor is participating in capitalism by starting a business. Essentially, Billy has made himself an indentured servant for years to come when he ~~fell~~ decided to go into debt.

Laws make student loan debt one of the best investments on the planet. That is for the loaner of the money, not the student! Non-dischargeable in bankruptcy plus a government guarantee (if you die before you pay off your loans, banks still get paid) makes me want to get into the business of offering student loans. If I owned a bank, I'd be out of lower-priced mortgages and trying to underwrite all the student loan business. Since prices keep rising and students want to take out more debt, and we can get their parents to sign up too — wow, even more customers, thanks, that's great! Great for banks, horrible for students. But I can't get into student loans because it's a government run monopoly.

If it were left to the free markets, then loans to students would be limited to the value of the degree received, less the risk factor. With up to 39% of Americans defaulting on their student loans, free markets would quickly change how much lenders would loan to students. But it is not a free market, it is a ~~market~~ monopoly controlled by the federal government.

Universities can continue to charge more only because loans are available. The biggest problem with the increase in the price of education is that the money is not for more educators and students are not getting a better education. More amenities, more sports programs, more things that don't matter, and a lot more of one thing that *does* matter —citizens shackled by debt.

A brief lesson in history – the financial system in America has never been set up to help the common man. We started with land ownership and indentured servants then moved quickly to slavery. Capital became so concentrated that in the 1870s, a few families controlled roughly 90% of the wealth in the US. The financial systems and financial education are not set up to help ordinary citizens; the rules are set up to favor the wealthy. After all, who do you think wrote the rules?

How we got here in the student loan crisis:

The 1965 Higher Education Act created loan programs. The original intent was to allow more people the opportunity of education by using some debt to get a degree. In 1976, the law was changed because a few congressmen were scared into believing that doctors were going to try to discharge their debts in bankruptcy. Yes, the same doctors who are one of the most likely groups to repay their loans was the starting point for making loans non-dischargeable in bankruptcy.

In 1984, under Reagan, among other handouts to big banks, the laws were changed to make all private student loans non-dischargeable in bankruptcy. So, not only are the loans backed by the government non-dischargeable, but all private loans are non-dischargeable as well. This led to more and more lenders offering private loans to students because they are guaranteed investments. While this increased loan availability, it was not good for students.

Then, in 2005, as part of the rewrite of the Bankruptcy Code, which made it harder to walk away from any debts, the laws made student loans excluded explicitly from bankruptcy – ***Special Debt***. – See Section 523.

Under President Obama, almost all student loans come from the government. While Obama said that this would, "Improve the lives of our people for generations to come", I don't think it has worked out that way. The more the government has intervened, the higher tuition has soared and the worse the loan crisis has become.

It is always tricky to figure out the original intent of laws, as it is hard to know all the parties involved and to understand all the ideas and options presented. For the sake of argument, let us assume the government's original intentions were good, and that the student loan programs were created to help students obtain loans, so everyone had the opportunity to pursue additional education. If it did start that way, it didn't take long before special interest groups (banks) got involved, used scare tactics that doctors wouldn't repay to convince lawmakers to give them protections, which seem to have been effective in the 1970s. It didn't take the lobbyist long to get their loans guaranteed and as loan amounts were increased the crisis began to grow. Today, it is ~~a massive crisis~~ an epidemic.

It is hard to imagine that anyone ever thought loans would be going to 18-year-old children who have never had a job. Who would think it possible to spend $200,000 for a 4-year degree? Who would be willing to loan that amount?

Shouldn't there be limits and controls to protect student? Obviously. But do you see what is missing in this story? There is no one protecting students. Universities have lobbying, banks have lobbying, governments want more control and the entire education system is setup for those going to college. Who is looking out for students?

We can't let the increase in the price of tuition rest solely with the government. Schools have been more than willing to increase tuition and spend lots of money to continue to play the ranking game while not providing adequate value to the students. Everyone participating in this process bears some blame, but it starts with the government.

Stanford just released all the “harmful” words we are no longer supposed to write or say lest someone’s feelings be triggered. In a write up about the release it was noted that there are more administrators working at Stanford then there are students. Yeah, that’s right, that’s the bloat of the current university, not more professors, more administrators, more administrators that students!!

When the government made loans guaranteed, they shut out the free market. Free markets are much better at determining the price for goods and services. If student debts were dischargeable in bankruptcy like other debts, then loan amounts would be much lower because of the risk they would be discharged in bankruptcy. If students didn't have access to the additional amount of debt, then either there would be fewer students or schools wouldn't be allowed to continue to increase prices, or they wouldn't have enough customers.

The hard part for most of us is that we want everyone to have opportunities and we don't want the ability to take out a loan to prevent a student from reaching their dreams. But it's evident that without the free market participating, the government-controlled debt system has gotten way out of hand, and we are now feeling those the consequences. There will be fewer entrepreneurs and more people unhappy in their jobs and in their lives, as they have sold their future in the pursuit of their dreams. To make matters worse, it is the taxpayers of this country who will ultimately pay these debts, so we all lose.

There are no easy solutions to fix this crisis. For those who worked and paid for their school, it wouldn't be fair to eliminate the debts for all the students who decided to take on debt instead of work through school. If we make college free for everyone, then not everyone will be able to attend. Not everyone will be able to pursue their dreams as there will be a budget for education, and only the most qualified will be admitted. This is the case in every country where college is free. It is only free if you can get in, and that is not good for society when Hugh Herr doesn't get to go to school.

The wealthy don't care about any of this. If you are wealthy, the $120,000 - $200,000 for a degree is not a significant amount of money. In fact, the wealthy are likely to continue to contribute to the schools they attended, and that almost guarantees their children will also be admitted and attend an Ivy League school, whether they deserve to or not. The wealthy also tend to spend a significant amount of money on education each year, sending their children to private schools, many of which may charge tuition that is similar to college. When families have this much money, the cost is just not significant. But to all other American families, these debts are significant and have negative impacts on society. For many these loan can lead to hopelessness.

The only way to change the system for yourself is to understand it and make better decisions. It is unlikely the government will do anything to improve the system, after all, they have a very bad track record of fixing their prior mistakes.

Eventually, likely through new AI systems, education will be reformed. We showed the math, the additional earnings expectations versus investing the same money shows a value proposition somewhere between $40,000 to $50,000. Good luck getting tuition back down 50%.

What you can do is make an informed decision for yourself.

SUPPLEMENT 2

Sports and College

Sports in college is a personal subject for me. I received a scholarship to play basketball in college, but only after I went to community college. The scholarship offers for me coming out of high school were only for a portion of tuition to small, liberal arts schools. The amount of money offered was not enough to make any of those schools an affordable option. Because of my love of the game and the desire to pursue that dream further, I decided to first go to community college. I didn't realize this was a smart way to get college credits. As someone who has been through the system, I can speak to the benefits of being an athlete, but there are also a lot of pitfalls that I want to share with prospective athletes and their parents.

The first lesson is that as you go through the system, as an athlete, you realize that the system is not set up to take care of the athletes. Overall, the system lacks fairness, and your success or failure may depend on the opinion of one person (typically called coach). Once you receive an NCAA scholarship, it is only good for one year. That's right, one year. If you don't perform as expected, or even get hurt, they can reduce or eliminate your scholarship money. I've seen it happen. I've seen coaches take care of players and I've seen players pushed and thrown out of programs.

One of my teammates did not have a good season on the court his first year on the team. The coaches felt he underperformed and was not living up to his ability. They used other excuses to cut his scholarship money the following year. He showed up to practice every day and other players had more off the court problems but performed better. Sometimes, as in this case, coaches have a different idea of how a player will perform on their team versus what actually happens. When an athlete's performance is below expectations, often coaches will not want to take responsibility for their role and instead put all the blame on the athlete.

Coaches usually don't like to say any scholarship reduction was based on performance, but it always comes down to performance. In almost every sports program, the coach is paid to win games. They don't get fired when too few athletes graduate; they get fired when the team does not win.

Meanwhile, young athletes in college are going through a lot of developmental changes, trying to find themselves in life, in academics and in athletics. Performance should be expected to have varied outcomes. But again, coaches are paid to win, and winning seems to be very important to schools. I'm still conflicted on how this goes with education as often the two seem to contradict one another. The game is good, the pressure to win often contradicts sportsmanship and learning.

Playing basketball in college was my dream. For most athletes, that dream can end on any given day because of injury. Or at the end of any season when your eligibility ends, or when a more talented player is recruited. When you analyze the statistics, most athletes play their final game while in high school.

Parents of athletes, like the 94% with high school kids who think their child will graduate from college, have similar expectations for college scholarships. Forty percent of parents of high school athletes believe their child could get a scholarship, and a staggering 34% believe their child could go pro or make it to the Olympics. Unfortunately, the actual rates for those getting even a partial scholarship are 2%. Yes, 2%. That is how few slots are available and why it is so competitive.

In Chapter 10, we discussed the family and the family's role in supporting students. For student athletes, this can be very difficult. When you are the best player on the team in high school, it is a difficult transition to go back to being average, and it's easy to lose confidence. At some point for every athlete, the game is over. Even Tom Brady finally retired, and for most athletes, even if they have the talent to go pro, Father Time will end their career in their 30's. Gravity remains undefeated! For those athletes pursuing the college dream, when you get pushed out from the game you love when you are still physically capable, it can be crushing emotionally. Many athletes cannot make the transition from being the best player to a role player.

In addition, being a college athlete is a job. And it is your primary job. If you don't achieve success on the field, you risk losing your scholarship and it can be the end of playing the sport you love. If you don't get passing grades in the classroom, you can also lose your scholarship, but athletics is primary, and academics is secondary. Schools don't put their football team's graduation rate in the advertisements during games; they talk about championships and wins. Coaches are not paid to teach or paid based on the graduation rate, they are paid to win, and fired if they don't.

If you have a class you need for your major that takes place during practice time, you're not missing practice. It may delay your graduation, but that is your problem, not the coach's or the team's. You will miss classes for travel, and most schools will not supply you with tutors—those are typically for top football and men's basketball programs only. Your professors will not care that you are an athlete, and most of the time you won't get any special treatment. The *special* treatment is usually the recommendation to take easy classes that you can pass so you can stay eligible, but that's not helping you towards a degree and a career, that is just keeping you eligible to help win games.

In my first year on scholarship, we made it to March Madness (Division 2), the NCAA tournament where every basketball player dreams that his team will come together, go on a five-game winning streak, and hold a trophy over his head to end the season. Like many of the games, we lost a close one. Two weeks before the NCAA tournament, we played our final league games on the road, a Tuesday game and a Friday game. The following week we left on Tuesday and played in our conference tournament, then we left on Monday on to the NCAA tournament.

In total, over those three weeks, we were in class for two days. My father told me that missing class, which resulted in a drop in my GPA was an excuse, but I can tell you that in those three weeks, not a single person on the team, coaching staff, or athletic department was concerned about our classes and our grades. My grades fell to B's and C's from A's and B's, and some of my teammates ended up in summer school to stay eligible.

Being an athlete is a full-time job. Between individual workouts, team conditioning, practice, games, travel, mandatory study hall, team meetings, etc., you will not have much time during the season to do anything except go to class, study a little, and be an athlete. You will have a playbook to memorize and film to study. If you don't genuinely love the game, the competitiveness and degree of effort required will make the entire experience challenging. In short, it is not correct to call it a full-time job— it's a lifestyle. You are 100% committed to your sport first, and everything else, second. If you get hurt or your performance is not as expected, the next guy takes your spot, and you may never get your playing time back.

I cannot complain about how the athletic system worked out for me. I was on a full-ride scholarship for three years. I was lucky enough to find myself in a good situation for my talent and position, and my performance was better than expected. My last two years I spent as team captain and my final year I was first-team all-league. My coach never reduced my scholarship money, and in fact, the athletic department paid for an additional year of tuition for me so that I could complete all my MBA without taking out debt.

But very few of my fellow athletes got the same treatment. Most of my teammates did not graduate, something that, to this day, I consider a tragedy. The coaches rationalized that the college experience that athletes received, despite not getting a degree, was beneficial to them. I think we can and should do better.

College athletics is a business. The coaches get fired when the team loses, so winning is priority number one, regardless of what anyone says. To the coach, you are a member of the team that is responsible for him or her keeping their job. Your academics take second stage. That is not to say that the coaches don't care at all. Most coaches make just enough money to live, and most do care about their athletes and are former athletes themselves. But because they care, it does not mean it changes the priorities.

If the priorities were graduation of athletes first and that is what coaches were fired over, then I wouldn't be writing this for you. One of the things I am grateful for was that my parents had very little direct influence on my decision to continue to play sports. Basketball was not their dream for me. They did not pressure me to continue to play at any level, but they supported me emotionally in my pursuit of my dream. I mention this because many athletes feel pressured by their parents to continue playing. Whether for the goal of the scholarship, or pride of the family or parents, many athletes I know and played with did not have that same support structure. They had pressure, and that pressure never helped.

One of the main drivers of that pressure can be the amount of time and money that families spend on their child athletes, with the intention of that preparation as a pathway to an athletic scholarship. Many families spend massive amounts of money paying for camps, elite travel teams, and personal lessons, seeking any advantage they can get to try to help their child receive a college scholarship. The sad truth is most of that money would be better spent in a college savings account and the children competing in local leagues.

I have counseled many athletes over the years on being an athlete in college. For the kids who carry the passion for the game and love the experience of competition, they will likely achieve the same results without the private lessons and travel teams. While my parents were supportive emotionally, there was no family money to spend on private lessons or elite travel teams. I was happy to have shoes that were not falling apart, and I had my own job to pay for those after age 14.

One of my roommates in college had a different experience. He was a star high school athlete in basketball and baseball. He loved both sports and loved to compete, and his family spent most of the summers of his high school years traveling to baseball tournaments. He fully expected a full-ride scholarship for baseball. Then in his senior year, he tore his ACL. The scholarship offers went away. He went through rehab and spent a year at a community college where he tore his ACL again. At that point, he had to walk away from the game and changed his focus to academics.

He is now a CFO at a large healthcare company. We had lots of discussions, especially after college, about the experience of being an athlete versus just a student and the money that parents spend on the pursuit of the college scholarship. Because we lived together, he saw how much time I spent in my athletics lifestyle. I got to see how much free time he had to have a job and enjoy the college experience. He missed the games and the competition, but he did not miss the practices, the early morning conditioning, the travel or the grind of the season and the pressure to win games. We discussed how much money and time his family spent in his youth, as his parents would often travel to watch him play, spending their weekends and family vacations at hotels and baseball fields. It was difficult for the entire family when injury took away the dream.

If you are a family that loves sport and enjoys spending time on fields and courts, then I'm not going to tell you to stop. But what if the experience of playing in college, the cut-throat nature of sports and "win at all costs" mentality is not in your child's best interest? What if, like 99% of us, you will not go pro? Is it worth it? Is the pressure to win, the costs of all that effort, worth the scholarship goal? Perhaps the family money would be better spent on a college savings account, and you could just be a student in college and focus on academics.

The Sports Partial Scholarship Value Proposition

The dream of playing in college and professionally exists for most youth. We play our sport pretending to be Tom Brady or

Stephen Curry, winning championships. What young player doesn't want to be on TV, making the winning play of the game, when the crowd goes crazy, and they carry you off the field with a trophy? That all sounds amazing. But only one team gets to win their final game. (Yes, I know that bad teams that don't make the playoffs could win their final game, but that doesn't count.) One team per year gets that ultimate dream.

I was lucky enough to raise a regional trophy in high school. We won the semifinal and final games by one point each. It took the school 25 years to win another and when they did, they interviewed our coach, who instead of praising us, said it wasn't his best team, the team the year before was better. That was not true; we were a much better team the year we won—he just didn't like us.

Welcome to sports, it is not the celebration you see on television; it is a complicated, competitive mess. I scored 22 of our 41 points in that championship game, and Coach still hates me! I never played for him; I played for my teammates and myself, and that was good because it was a lesson for me about coaches. They can be selfish, and often view the win as part of "their record," they just don't say that when they are recruiting you. When their job is on the line, they can also become very different people.

What is also lost inside the dream at many schools is that most of the athletes are on partial scholarships. Many of my teammates were, and in sports besides football and men's basketball, often the entire team is on a partial scholarship, as the scholarships can be limited except at the largest schools. So, here is the dangerous part, the partial scholarship that leaves the family with a value proposition, especially at liberal arts schools.

The value proposition goes like this: tuition usually is $40K per year, but because you are an athlete, we will give you a $25K per year scholarship. What a deal! Except wait a minute, that means the family still must come up with $15,000 a year in tuition and more for room and board. As discussed, this is a lifestyle, so there is no time for a job; the NCAA may even forbid you to have a job or internship. So, athletes and their families take out loans just like everyone else, and next thing you know, $75K to $100K of debt while ON SCHOLARSHIP. That is the kind of offer that sounds great when you only tell someone half of the information: "My daughter got a $25K scholarship to University." "Wow, how wonderful for her! You must be so proud!" (What they don't share is that the actual cost was an equal amount, and it was not such a great scholarship after all!)

I have a friend who had this recently happen to his daughter. She believed she could play in the Olympics one day. That was the dream. She was offered a rugby scholarship similar to the "wonderful" offer above, and she accepted. She got some additional financial help from the family and a few other academic scholarships. Still, she graduated with over $70K of debt, had two knee surgeries, and she will not be competing in the Olympics. Was it worth it? That's not for me to say.

If you can't tell based on my story, I love the pursuit of dreams. People telling me I couldn't was great motivation to prove them wrong and helped me to achieve my dreams, but I was lucky enough to be able to do the math. Since I detest debt, instead of accepting a similar offer, I chose the less expensive route. The one without debt. My friend's daughter could have lived at home, gone to community college, and got the same degree at the local state school and graduated with little or no debt. But the family got sold on the "value proposition" that she was getting a great deal because the scholarship amount meant that she paid so much less than the sticker price of tuition. I hope she had a wonderful time competing. I hope to ask her one day when the loans are all paid off if the loans were worth the experience. That is a lot of her future earnings trapped within the "value proposition".

To all the athletes and families of athletes out there, please go back to Chapter 2 and remember the ***why***. The ***why*** of college is for the degree and the opportunity it affords, not debt, not athletic glory. Be realistic about your opportunity to turn pro, and even if you are lucky enough to make it there, know that you need an education for what comes after 35, when 99% of professional athletes are retired. Tom Brady is a unicorn. Maybe you can make it 40 like Vince Carter, but odds are you will be done being paid for playing before 30 if you do go pro. For the rest of us, the pay stops when the college or high school career ends.

Know that when you are offered a partial scholarship that you still need to consider the rest of the cost. Don't end up deep in debt because you got sold on some "great" value proposition.

Please don't pressure an athlete to keep playing if they are not interested in the lifestyle because if your heart's not in it, it can drive you to hate the game you used to love. I saw this too many times and don't wish that experience on anyone.

Also, be aware of your physical self, especially football players. The injuries from sports can last a lifetime. I consider myself fortunate that the only surgery I need from sports was to fix a deviated septum. Many athletes have multiple knee, ankle, hip and back problems that result in many surgeries and physical pain for years to come. Some injuries last a lifetime. There is no compensation for this from the schools, it is another hidden cost that the athlete must bear.

SUPPLEMENT 3

The Forms

In order to receive Federal and Statey money available to you, including Pell Grants and other need-based financial aid and even loans, families must fill out the FAFSA form. It is online, and the website walks you through the process. Here is what you need upfront:

Gathering the Documents Needed to Apply

The FAFSA questions ask for information about you (your name, date of birth, address, etc.) and about your financial situation. Depending on your circumstances (for instance, whether you're a US citizen or what tax form you used), you might need the following information or documents as you fill out the application:

1. Your Social Security number (it's important that you enter it correctly on the FAFSA form!)
2. Your parents' Social Security numbers if you are a dependent student
3. Your driver's license number if you have one
4. Your Alien Registration number if you are not a US citizen
5. Federal tax information or tax returns including IRS W-2 information, for you (and your spouse, if you are married), and for your parents, if you are a dependent student:

» IRS 1040

» Foreign tax return, IRS 1040NR, or IRS 1040NR-EZ

- » Tax return for Puerto Rico, Guam, American Samoa, the US Virgin Islands, the Marshall Islands, the Federated States of Micronesia, or Palau

A. Records of your untaxed income, such as child support received, interest income, and veterans noneducation benefits, for you, and for your parents, if you are a dependent student

B. Information on cash; savings and checking account balances; investments, including stocks and bonds and real estate (but not including the home in which you live); and business and farm assets for you, and your parents if you are a dependent student

SUPPLEMENT 4

Out-of-State Tuition Hacks

As previously stated, going to school out-of-state is not recommended, but since I did it, I can't say it shouldn't be done, and my story is one of the better ways to do it. Don't think that was intentional and give my younger self too much credit; my focus was on extending my basketball career at the lowest possible cost in the pursuit of a scholarship, which just happened to lead me on the out-of-state path, twice.

Another disadvantage of being out of state is that you are usually not eligible for governor's grants. Those are typically reserved for in-state students. So, in addition to higher tuition, you qualify for less aid.

If you are going to go out of state, then first you need to know the rules. You can get residency in a different state; all you need to do is move there and act like a resident. Pay taxes, register your car, get a driver's license, and register to vote. That's the minimum if you are serious.

The rules continue to get stricter because of the amount of money on the line for the schools trying to collect the out-of-state tuition. As mentioned, Oregon has the largest student body of out-of-state students, and that is by design. The University of California system has seven of the ten highest costs for out-of-state tuition in addition to one of the strictest standards to become a resident.

Since California was where I received in-state residency and it is one of the hardest residencies to get, we will use that as the example. The easiest way to get residency is to move immediately after high school to the state in which you want to live. You will likely need to take a gap year if you want the most savings.

Typically, after one year (if you move in June or July and enroll the following August), the community college will treat you as an in-state resident. But if you don't follow all the rules, they will use any of them—no job, no taxes paid, no driver's license, no car registration, etcetera—as reasons to deny you in-state tuition. Give them no reasons to reject you. Act like a citizen of the state, and your tuition will be a lot cheaper.

I learned these rules the easy way because I was an athlete. During the summer after graduating high school, I was on campus for basketball camps, where we got paid, and we started the "process" to help us become residents. This allowed me to receive a Governor's grant in my second year.

The institutions have "residency applications," and they tell you what documentation you need to provide, including: a driver's license, California tax returns, registration of vehicles owned in California, bank account at a California branch, voter registration. Everything needs to have a California address on it, including FAFSA forms. The other important factor is intent – you have to believe it for it to be true and believing it does not mean you cannot move back home or somewhere else after school, but don't talk about it. Your story needs to be consistent as a resident.

One other thing that often catches students and parents. If you are moving to California to be a resident at 18, then your parents need to stop claiming you as a dependent. This could cost a few hundred dollars of tax savings, but it is included in the questionnaire, so it's important. If you intend to become a resident, then you cannot remain a dependent in another state. After 18, the child tax credit is irrelevant, so the tax advantage is limited versus the cost of out-of-state tuition.

As an athlete, we had an assistant coach who went over all these things with us so we could plan for them. Most students won't start the process for the following year until they arrive on campus, but that is too late as schools usually require "a year and a day" as the residency standard. So far, I'm discussing the community college standard. The University of California system standard is two years, so going to community college is a *must* if you want to go out-of-state to California.

If you have a job, a residence you pay rent year-round, and you are filing taxes in the state you have moved to, most community colleges will treat you as a resident after one year. However, you need to ask so you know the rules. This is very important if you don't want to take a gap year. If you can take the gap year, then doing so will mean you pay in-state tuition immediately. But for community college, sometimes the additional tuition is manageable, so you can enroll immediately but move to a resident status after one year. This is what I did as I wanted to register immediately. After one year, they changed my status to in-state. Again, I had an athlete advantage to make this happen, so it is a good idea to talk to a counselor and explain your situation to determine the best path forward.

Once I was determined to be a resident, then I was eligible for a governor's grant, which I received, and used to pay for tuition and books. Because of the governor's grant, my second year of school tuition was free. My first year I used the money I earned from my job because tuition was affordable because it was a community college. Keeping my room and board expenses low allowed me to get through the first two years of community college without taking out any debt. Then I was lucky enough to receive a basketball scholarship in Colorado. But had that not worked out, I would have been a California resident able to attend any of the state schools as an in-state resident and eligible for governor's grants.

This is the only affordable way to go out of state. It may require a gap year and two years at community college to ensure in-state tuition when you transfer. Once a California school, even a community college, has determined you meet the in-state residency requirements, usually all other schools you transfer to will accept that in-state classification so long as you continue to live, work and file taxes in that state.

***

I have a friend, Peter, who went to Penn State. Peter was from New Jersey, where about half of high school graduates go out of state for college. He was lucky to have family support to help with most of the costs. He spent his freshman year partying and was surprised to learn that many people he met at parties did not attend Penn State, but instead went to the community college. Had Peter and his family decided to take a gap year or even just attend the community college for two years, he could have saved about $60K in out of state tuition. His degree would have been the same and many of the experiences, too. How would life be different for Peter if he graduated with $60K in his bank account instead of student loans? Peter says it would have been a significant financial head start, but he didn't consider it because going immediately to school and paying out-of-state tuition was what half of his classmates did.

This is the story I hear the most, students are making their decisions based on what their classmates are doing. Financial implications are secondary. These decisions, based on emotions, are a large reason there is a crisis today.

If you are determined to leave home, I understand, but there are smart ways and expensive ways to go about it. Getting residency is a game with rules—know the rules, play the game. Community college credits count the same, and many schools are in smaller towns with a much lower cost of living than cities. Take advantage of those opportunities to help reduce any amount of debt you are thinking of taking on and know that in-state classification also makes you eligible for governor's grants that you can't get if you are an out-of-state student.

There is no way that anyone can convince me that spending an extra $100K plus on out of state tuition is worthwhile. It is simply a waste of family resources. You would never spend that difference on any other purchase, imagine spending an extra $100K on a Honda Accord so you could tell everyone you bought it in California! Why would it be worth it on a degree? It won't. Take the gap year or stay in your home state for school.

Fixing the Current Problem

After spending too many hours researching the causes of student loan debt, its impacts on people's lives, and arguing with those who just want everyone to receive forgiveness, I've heard a lot of ideas for fixing this system and come up with a few of my own. Tradeoffs everywhere!

Can Congress get past the influence of special interest groups to fix this system? I'm hopeful, but it is a difficult thing to admit you're wrong and get past the influence of those who contribute to your campaigns. This problem was, is and continues to be a problem created by Congress. A company will usually fire the person responsible for poor leadership, unfortunately, that is harder to do with government. Rarely is anyone ever held accountable and unfortunately, they also don't have to bear the consequences of their poor decisions.

A recent WSJ article, *Is the US Student Loan Program Facing and $500 Billion Hole? One Banker Thinks So,* sheds some light on another part of this problem that must be addressed when considering the solution: it is likely that a lot of current debt will never be repaid. If we know people cannot afford to pay the debt, then it seems cruel to keep those people trapped in debt for the rest of their lives.

To fix this crisis, the first measure is to limit future damage by having the same events occur that have led us down this path. This means limiting the amount of loans the government will guarantee. If we limited the amount of all debt to say, $7,000 per year, then the total student loan debt burden would be capped. Those currently in control will say this will limit opportunities, but really what it will cause is schools to eliminate everything not required for teaching. Schools can do this, they can get back to what education should be about, teachers (preferably Tenured Professors) and a room to meet in. All the stadiums, fancy gyms, lazy river apartments and such can go by the wayside and all the administrators can go do something useful instead of stealing money from young adults. This is the part that the vested interest groups will have the hardest time agreeing to as it will take away the piggy bank from the administrators.

If future debt could be limited, we can address current debts. If we don't first fix the future, forgiving current debt as we described in the Morehouse forgiveness for the class of 2019, a debt jubilee will only help today's graduates and not prevent the same situation tomorrow. If we are not going to fix the problem, then let's mandate a real education course on debt before anyone can get a loan. Most education of loans comes with the first payment requirement and that is a little late.

There is another good argument for debt forgiveness: many students were sold a false bill of goods. In an article for the NY Times, Tressie McMillan Cottom makes a good argument that many parents and students were sold a false bill of goods when it came to the benefits of a college education. As we mentioned with the high debts at Morehouse College, minority students tend to graduate with higher levels of debt. While I disagree with Ms. Cottom's conclusion that all debt should be forgiven immediately, I agree with the argument that a false bill of goods has been sold. That sales pitch comes from the entire education system. For those who can afford to repay their debts and are earning higher salaries, making taxpayers pick up the tab seems unfair to taxpayers.

Current debts can be adjusted in a few different ways. The first is allowing, after a reason time period of 3-5 years, for student loan debts to be discharged in bankruptcy. This will allow those who are and have been in default without future income prospects to limit the amount they will have to pay and eventually have remaining debt forgiven. This is not intended to be a free pass to everyone, and for those who are earning more from their degrees, they should contribute to repayment, but not for life.

Practically, this would be a judge's decision on each case. If you can afford to continue to pay, like a doctor or my friend with an MBA, for example, you should. But if you are already in default without a higher paying job, your debt can be reduced or eliminated. Another easy to way do this is to make student loan payments a percentage of income for a set period of years (10% of income for 10 years sounds about right). This should not be a continuing plan, as if there continue to be large amounts of debt after 10 years of 10% repayments, then tuition is still too high. At some point, we have to limit the cost if we are going to limit the payments.

The percentage of income idea has been around for some time, often as a solution unto itself by asking the universities to fund their own students. What if all students at any school could agree to this and the school only got the money from these students for the next 10 years? The schools would then have a big stake in who they admit as they would need to recoup those costs and if students didn't graduate, they would likely get a lot less money. I don't expect schools would take on this type of risk, they would rather the students continue to have all the risk.

Having the education institutions be responsible for some student debt would put the incentives back in the right place. Currently, schools want you to enroll and pay, at that point their job in sales in done. But if they didn't get their money or were forced to repay some in the future because a student cannot repay the loan, that would be a real incentive to change the culture. It would be about the life of the student, making what they learn and what skills they develop much more important. It would make teaching of important skills that are needed by employers more relevant. I can see the argument against this as but as much effort is already put into admissions, it seems reasonable many schools could become more of partners with their students.

Limiting the time for repayment would also solve situation where students have made payments totaling more than their loan amounts, but still owe more than when they got out of school. The defined period and percentage would essentially make this a "fair" repayment program with everyone paying based on their ability. While 10 years is a long time, it makes school look more like an indentured servant program and less like economic slavery, which is the current appearance.

In addition to limiting the repayment period the government could immediately lower the interest rate on all current debt. While the WSJ article shows the government actually views the student loan program as a revenue stream, we can see from the defaults it is not, so why not acknowledge reality and treat the future workers of this country as well as you do the big banks? They get to borrow for free, while students pay 7% or more?

This will surely leave another budget hole, but no more than already exists if the government were forced to fairly value the current loans based on expected defaults. It also sounds like a system instead of just arbitrary forgiveness that seems like vote buying. It would also be a good first step to acknowledging the actual cost of government intervention and passing laws to get the government out of education.

Importantly, it is not just a free handout to everyone of $10,000, it is a fair program for paying back a percentage of your salary and Congress needs to admit that this was their fault, and this is the fairest way to fix the problem they created. If the private sector had remained the sole place for loans, and they were dischargeable in bankruptcy, none of this would have come to pass. Loans would have been limited based on expected earnings from each degree and the person guaranteeing the loan, instead the current system of giving families however much they want for any degree regardless of ability to repay.

The group of people that need the most attention for debt forgiveness are those who have student loans and no degree. That lack of degree means their likelihood of earning more based on their education is unlikely and therefore the burden of those loans is much more negatively impactful. To those who did not finish school we should base forgiveness based on their current salary or allow for a specific bankruptcy proceeding to discharge this debt and not affect their credit score. It is fair to say that many students and parents were sold a lie. The statistics in the number of parents who believe their kids will graduate from college versus the reality tells that story. College is not for everyone, telling everyone so needs to stop. This Epidemic won't end without changing public perceptions.

Solutions like these are included in a category of items that I like to call a Big Ask. It is a Big Ask for the government to admit they were wrong and created the student loan crisis (even though the facts show this is clearly the case).

It is a Big Ask for special interest groups, including school administrators and the entire university system, to admit their exploitation of students by increasing costs while students bear the debt burden.

It is a Big Ask for there to be education on debt and the future cost of repayment before loans are granted.

It is a Huge Ask to actually get Congress to pass a law that just makes people's lives better and returns systems to the free market.

For the one million Americans who default on their loans each year and for all the former students who live with their student loans hanging over their financial freedom, I hope this Big Ask can be accomplished. It would give everyone struggling under their debt burden hope of a future not encumbered by student loan debt. No one should have their social security checks garnished for student loans.

It must be the disconnect from being in school, when all the debt is taken out, and out of school by the time it comes to repayment that prevents students from acting today. In the 1960's campus protests were normal. Students were fighting for civil rights and against war and the draft. They were right on both! Why are students' today not protesting daily at the high number of administrators? Forced teaching on ideologies that defy reality and science? and the high debt burdens from overpriced tuition?

Students are willing to show up at the Supreme Court to ask judges to allow an illegal forgiveness of the loans they committed to, but can't get out on their own campus to protest the costs they were gouged to begin with? And the Supreme Court judges who agree with the Constitution are the bad people? Not the administrators who lied to you about Aid and overcharged you for all the administrators they hired? Seems obvious this energy should be redirected back on campus.

Protests in Germany just shut down all transportation. Literally, no trains running. Imagine if students could get together and all decide not to sign up for classes one semester, even if just at one school and just one grade of students. Sophomores', everyone take 2nd semester off and say you will not come back until tuition is reduced and most administrators fired! Demand open debate a return to science. What a site that would be!

The woke mob can be turned back against those that created it. What if the real scientists were able to get rid of the woke in the same way they have been attacked? How about some open tribunals on campus where science and open debate about what is being taught can be held? Tenure may have been a good idea to protect different ideas, but it may also have run too far in guaranteeing crazy people can keep teaching crazy ideas. Ideological ideas, not science. If you don't believe we are binary, and women and men see the world differently and are biologically different, then you should not be teaching. Testosterone is real, and so are narcissistic men who want privileges they don't deserve by calling themselves women. And I'm happy to debate this topic at any time with anyone because teaching we are non-binary is absolute insanity. Teaching Marxism without acknowledging that every time it has been tried in history it has resulted in thousands, if not millions, of people killed is disingenuous. Denying that incentives matter is so silly it makes my dog laugh.

The current system may require complete destruction and a rebuilding. Campus should be a lot of students and a few professors (who actually believe in and follow science and the pursuit of knowledge) and as few administrators as possible. Sports teams should all be secondary, in the spirit of competition. The Latin for compete is *competere*, defined as "to strive in common". Coaches as the highest paid state employees, universities with huge stadiums and players receiving barely anything is not stiving in common, its exploitation.

I, nor you, can fix all of these problems that have created this crisis, and it is very unlikely government will do anything worthwhile, but you can prevent yourself from taking out debt. Just say no.

Artificial Intelligence Impacts to Education

Artifical Intelligence has quickly become part of the lexicon and its impacts are going to be similar to the personal computer and the internet. Advances in chip technologies are allowing supercomputers to process more data and with the release of Chat GPT, Bard and other language learning models, the public is now seeing what researches have been working on for years.

The future of technology and the impacts of AI are very reminiscent of the late 1990's, when the internet was to disrupt all things. While it took longer than promised, as most things do, we can now see the profound effects: you have a supercomputer in your pocket that also works as a phone, camera, camcorder, microphone, speaker, MP3 player and more. Social media and internet shopping have changed the way we communicate and purchase goods. AI will have a similar impact, if not greater.

The education market is ripe for change, it must change, for many of the reasons discussed in this book. The problem many people have is they want to see the path to change when that path is not knowable. However, the technology is now very apparent, and despite the best efforts of those in charge, education is going to change.

AI can already put together a better syllabus and coursework than most professors. Additional models will be able to tailor that teaching to your learning style. YouTube currently gives you videos to watch, but now imagine those videos and additional curriculum are made specifically for you, based on what you know, how you learn and designed to keep you engaged and to retain the skills you want to learn.

This future is closer than we think. As a though experiment, let's work backwards. First, imagine an AI system that is being fed the inputs of work requirements for an engineer. As the AI system is trained on the outputs and the work process, it identifies the skills needed along the way. Instead of multiple professors at a university each designing their own curriculum that may or may not be useful in learning those skills, the AI system develops a program that includes all the skills required by the future job.

A separate AI system is trained to learn about you. How you learn, giving you tests not to give you a grade, but to determine how you best retain information. It takes in all the information from your personality as well as how you perform depending on how information is presented. It learns you and what works best for you. It likely will also know what tasks you may enjoy the most and can recommend to you a job with those type of tasks.

You could then look at the jobs available in that field, or AI might know those already, and it would be likely that an employer would hire you if you had the skills necessary. Based on what jobs are available and your interests, the AI system now creates a specific training course for you.

Personalized education, with a constant tutor, giving you the education you need to learn the skills required in the most accessible way for you to learn. This is the potential of AI in education.

Take this thought experiment back to the employer. Instead of references from a professor or discussing which degree you have, the AI system can relay what you know to a future employer. The education course could be one specifically approved or even designed by that employer. This is not a stretch of the imagination; it already happened in technology. The university systems could not keep up with the rapid changes in software programming, so Google, Microsoft and others created their own certifications that became more valuable than degrees in programming.

The cost of university degrees against a backdrop of personalized learning has the potential to make the university system unnecessary. While a lot of academics will still want to get together to discuss theory, the value proposition of a university degree will no longer retain the same value.

Just as cars took a long time to replace horses, and computers took a long time to replace all the typewriters, AI will take time to replace the universities. How long that will take is guesswork. However, just as technology moved faster than universities in teaching programming, AI will move faster at teaching and assessing job skills that employers need. The education systems themselves are likely to be developed by businesses to teach the skills to workers directly.

Ironically, the cost structure of college opens the door more than ever for disruptive technology to step in because the cost benefit has become so distorted. The cost to build AI systems to do the things mentioned will be high, but when allocated across so many students, the cost to provide the services will be much less than a current degree and tailored specifically to the student, something universities will never be able to offer.

The future is a better educational product at a much lower cost to you. Something to consider before spending $100,000 or more and taking on long term debt for a degree that may not be very valuable in the near future.

Made in the USA
Monee, IL
13 September 2026

62981963R00152